BEFORE YOU BEGIN

PARTS OF THE GUITAR

This book is designed to be used with any type of six-string guitar: acoustic, nylon string, or electric. Each video included with the book may show a certain type of guitar, but any kind of guitar can be used for every exercise or song. This is because although there are a few key differences all guitars share many of the same parts.

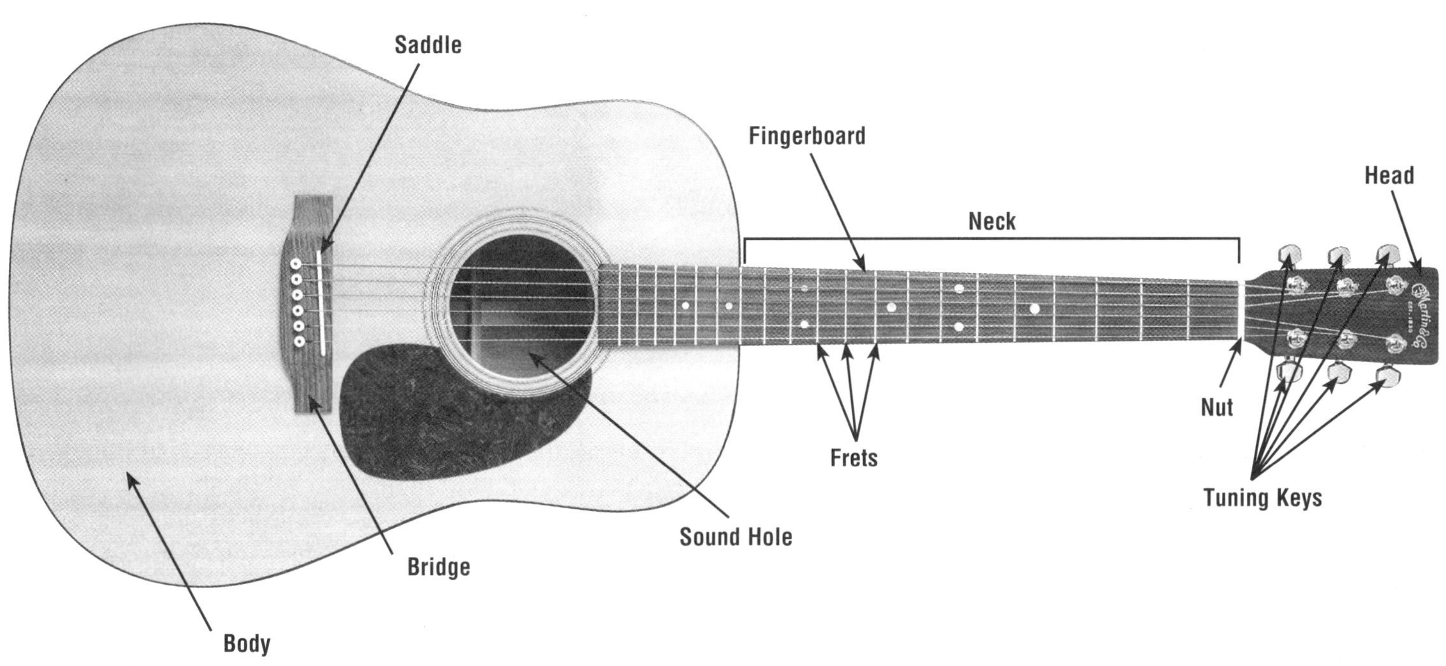

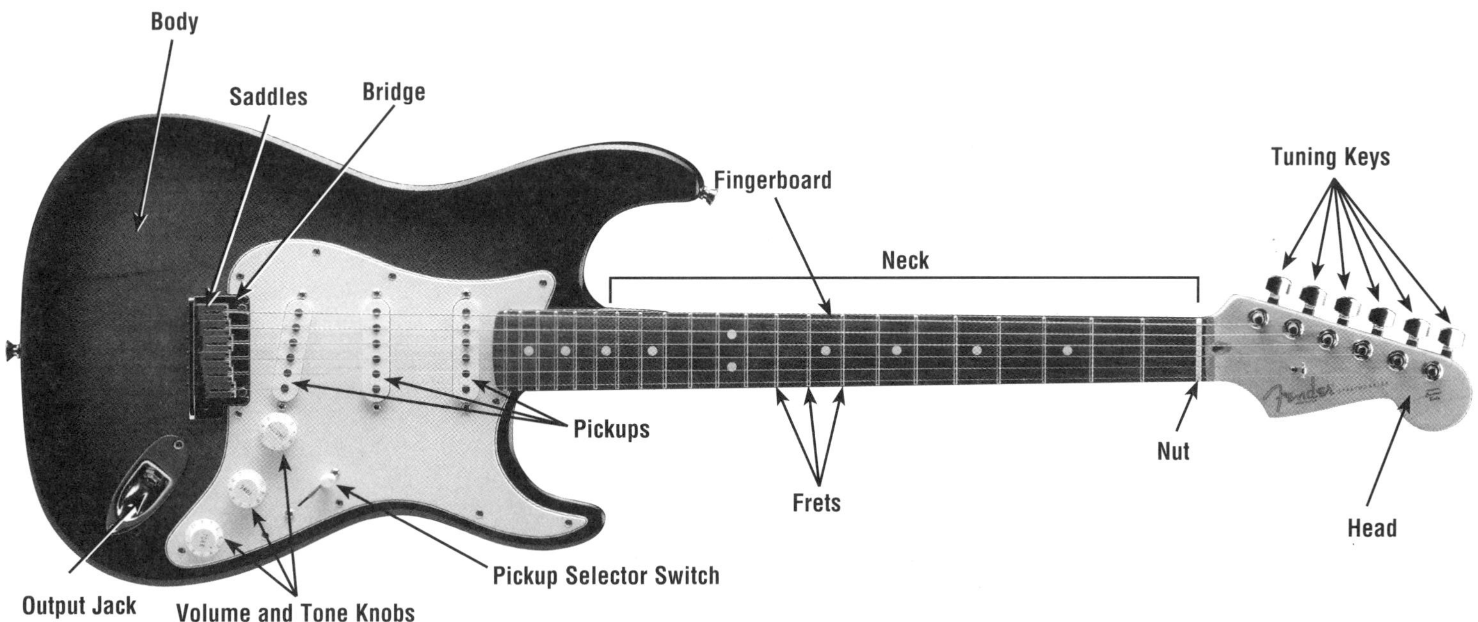

TUNING THE GUITAR 

The easiest and most accurate way to tune your guitar will be to use an electronic tuner or one of the many free tuner apps that can be downloaded to your device. All tuners will read the pitch of the string, and a meter or arrows will tell you which way to adjust the string to put it in tune. If the string is "flat" (or sounds lower than the correct pitch), you'll need to tighten the corresponding tuning key to bring up the pitch. If your string is "sharp" (or sounds too high), you'll need to loosen the tuning key to bring it down. When finished, compare your notes to the ones on the featured audio.

HOLDING THE GUITAR

You can play the guitar sitting down or you can stand and use a strap. Either way, make sure your posture is loose and relaxed but not hunched over. Keep the guitar facing out while you play and avoid tilting the front up towards you in an effort to see it better.

HAL LEONARD GUITAR METHOD

GUITAR FOR TEENS

A Beginner's Guide with Step-by-Step Instruction for Acoustic and Electric Guitar

BY DOUG BODUCH

To access audio & video, visit:
www.halleonard.com/mylibrary
Enter Code
3589-5554-8437-1961

ISBN 978-1-7051-5433-5

Visit Hal Leonard Online at
www.halleonard.com

World headquarters, contact:
Hal Leonard
7777 West Bluemound Road
Milwaukee, WI 53213
Email: info@halleonard.com

In Europe, contact:
Hal Leonard Europe Limited
Dettingen Way
Bury St Edmunds, Suffolk, IP33 3YB
Email: info@halleonardeurope.com

In Australia, contact:
Hal Leonard Australia Pty. Ltd.
4 Lentara Court
Cheltenham, Victoria, 3192 Australia
Email: info@halleonard.com.au

INTRODUCTION

Welcome to *Guitar for Teens*! This book is designed for young adults who want to learn to play guitar, whether it's acoustic or electric. You'll learn to read standard music notation as well as guitar tablature (or tab) by playing songs you actually know, from classic rock to today's hits. The songs and exercises included come with online video or audio examples, so you can see and hear exactly how it's done. You'll learn essential musical concepts and cool guitar techniques—I packed a lot into this book, really everything I've been doing with my teenage students for the last 30 years!

—Doug Boduch

ABOUT THE AUDIO AND VIDEO

Throughout this book, examples with accompanying video are marked with a video icon. When an audio track is included instead, you'll see an audio icon. Go to **www.halleonard.com/mylibrary** and enter the code found on page 1 of this book to instantly access every accompanying audio and video file. You can either download the files to your device or stream the audio and video in real time. You can also use our PLAYBACK+ multi-functional audio player to slow down or speed up the tempo, change keys, or set loop points—a feature available exclusively from Hal Leonard, included with the price of this book!

HAND POSITION

We generally keep the thumb behind the neck to support the fingers. When playing, keep the hand relaxed and the fingers arched, and strive to place just the fingertips on the strings.

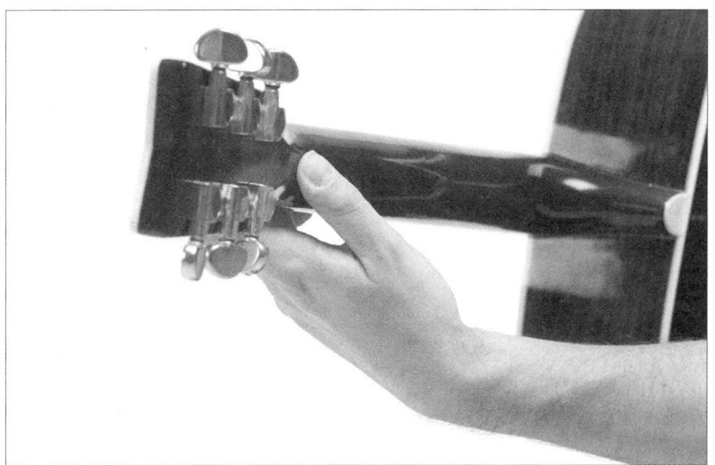

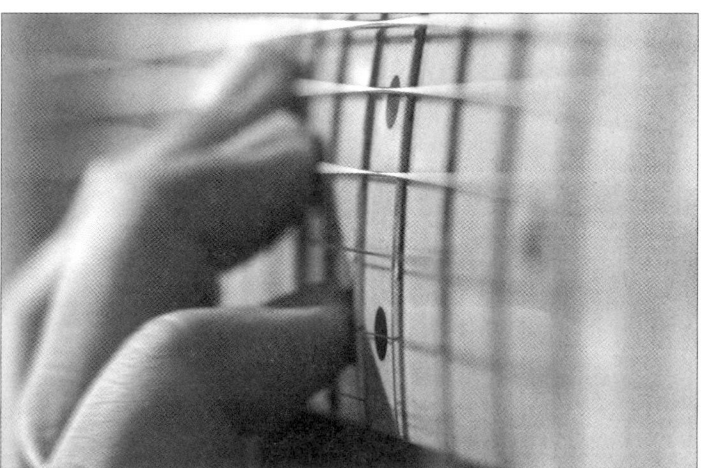

Most of the time we'll be playing with a pick. Hold it between your thumb and the side of your index finger, as shown in the photo.

Here's what correct right-hand position looks like from the player's perspective. The exact position will vary a bit from player to player, and it will also depend on whether we're picking just one string or strumming multiple ones. Whatever the case, this photo gives you a good starting point.

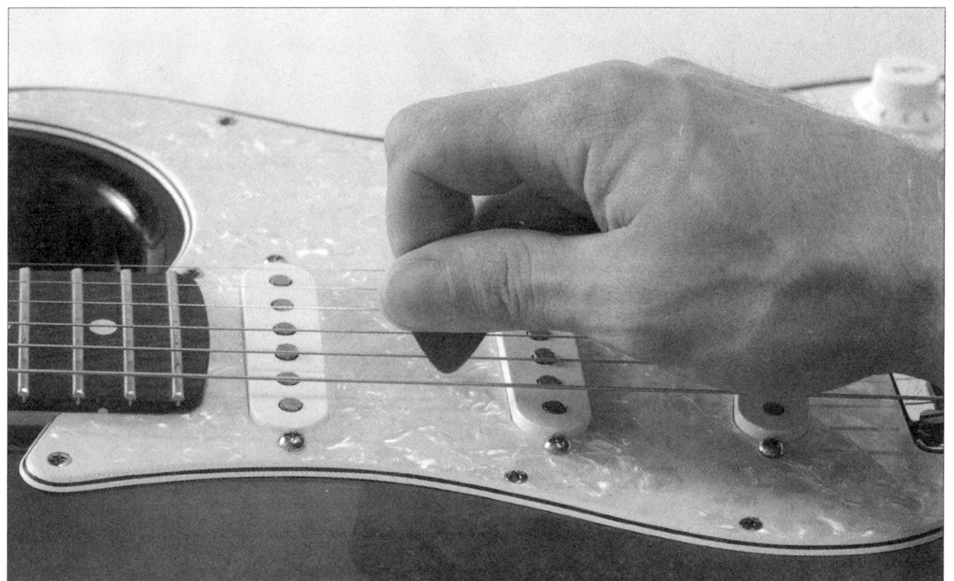

READING TABLATURE

In this book, we'll use standard notation along with a system of notation known as *tablature*, or "tab" for short. Guitar tab includes six lines, one for each string. The sixth string (low E string) is at the bottom, and the first string (high E string) is at the top.

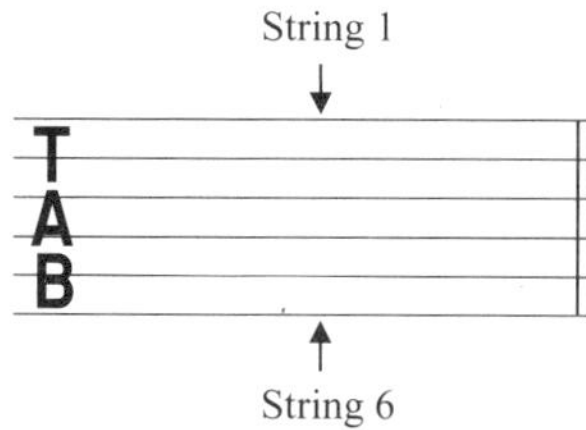

Numbers are placed on the lines to tell you which fret to play on the string. A "0" on a line means that you play that string "open" (un-fretted). The corresponding notes above the tab show the rhythms that go along with the tab numbers. We'll start talking about how to read rhythms right away in chapter 1.

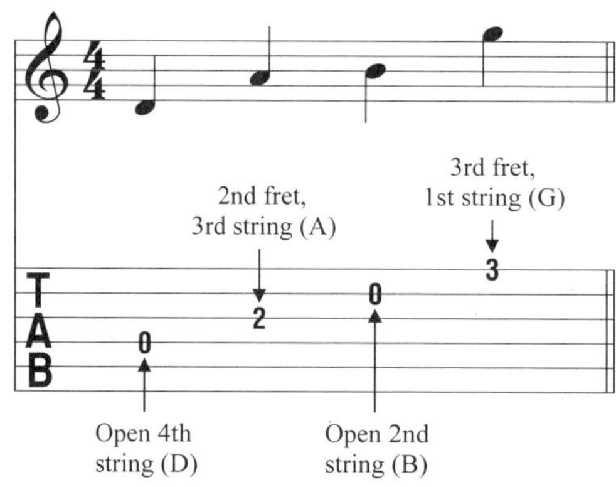

READING CHORD FRAMES

Chord frames, also known as *chord grids* or *chord diagrams*, show us how to play chords. We'll use these frames to teach single notes too. The vertical lines represent the strings, and the horizontal lines represent the frets. Black dots show us where to put our fingers, and numbers under each dot, below the frame, tell us which fingers to use. The fingers of the left hand are numbered 1 through 4.

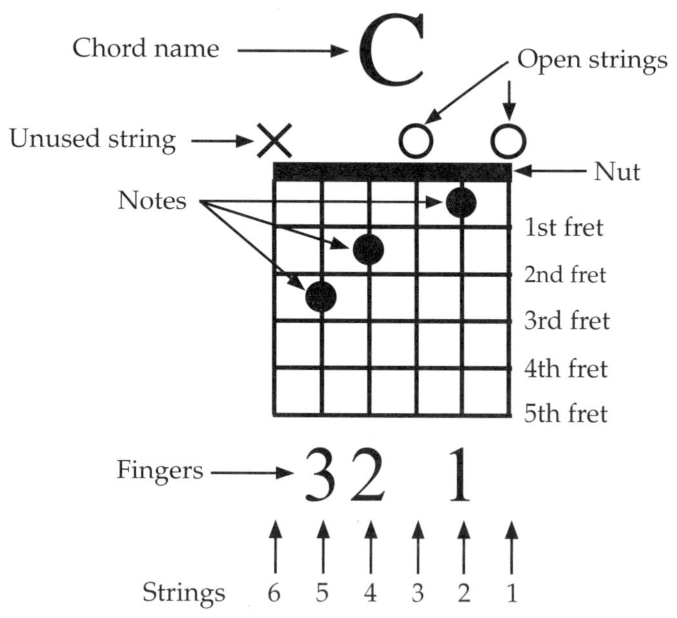

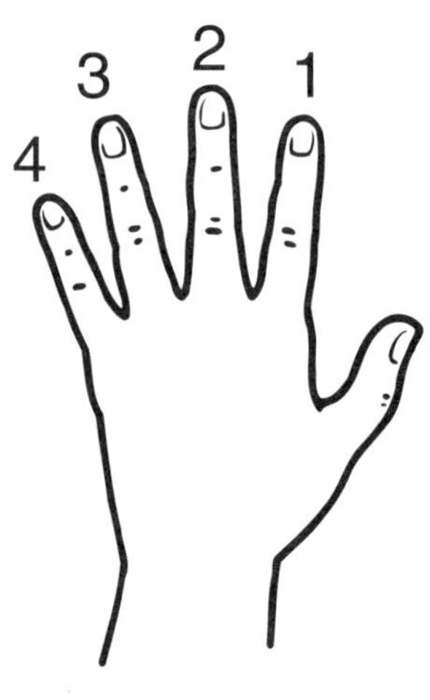

CHAPTER 1: NOTES ON THE FIRST THREE STRINGS

THE FIRST STRING

Let's start off by playing the first string "open," just like we did when we tuned it. We say that a string is played open when we simply pick the string with our right hand and don't use our left hand to hold down any notes. That note you get when playing the first string open is called an "E."

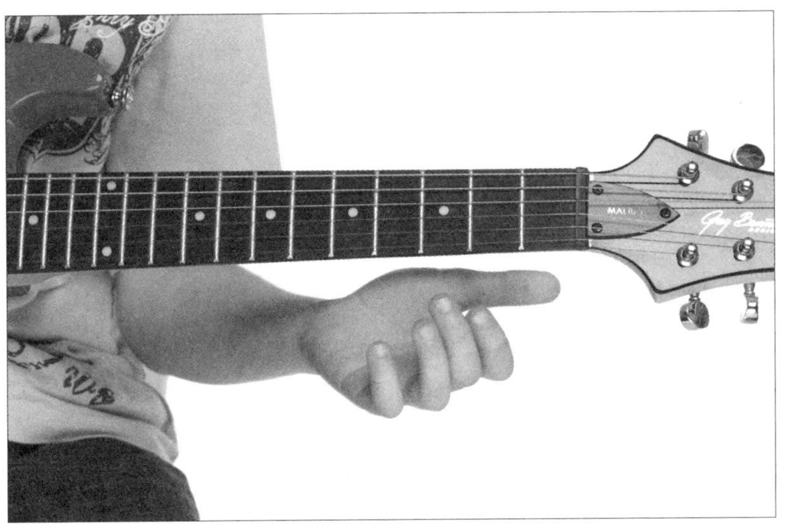

PITCH & RHYTHM

Music has two main ingredients: pitch and rhythm. *Pitch* is all about how high or low a note sounds. If you play your first string (the thin, highest-pitched string) and compare it to the sixth string (the thick, lowest-pitched string), you should be able to hear that the first string sounds higher. That's pitch. *Rhythm* has to do with the duration of a note, or how long it lasts. To create various rhythms, we combine different types of notes, each lasting for a certain number of beats. *Beats* are the pulses that we feel in music, where you might tap your feet to keep time.

In the first example, you played a *whole note*. This type of note lasts for four beats, meaning we can count "1-2-3-4" as we play it and hold the note for the full count. Start counting when you first pluck the string and then let the note sustain until you're done counting. Try playing a few more whole notes, this time counting up to "4" as you play each one. Check out the video and play along.

EXERCISE 1

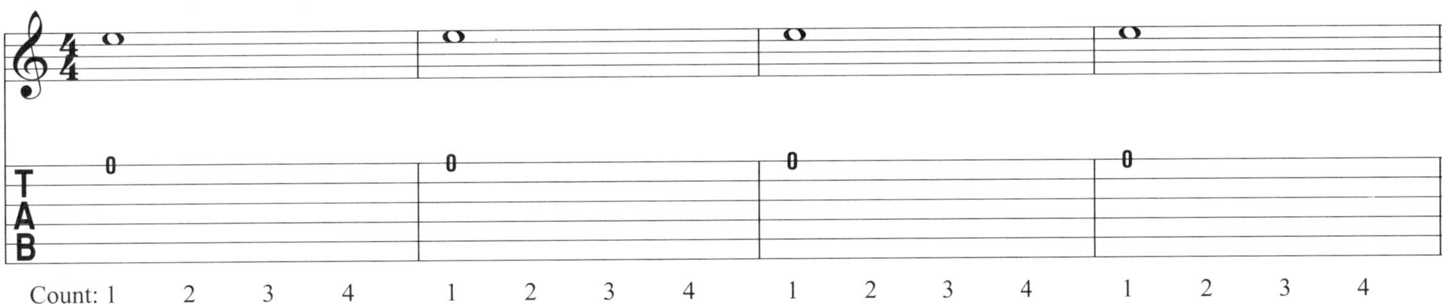

We can change up the rhythm a bit by playing half notes instead of whole notes. *Half notes* last for two beats and look like this…

EXERCISE 2

So, if you're good at math, you probably figured out that two half notes are equal in time (duration) to one whole note. Now try playing some half notes while counting along, 1-2-3-4. Again, play along with the video.

EXERCISE 3

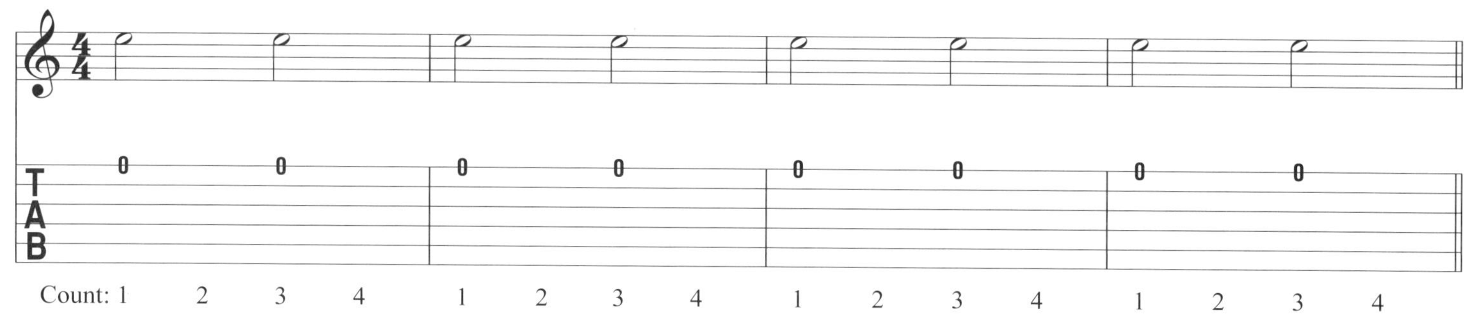

BAR LINES & MEASURES

Did you notice those vertical lines separating each pair of half notes? Those are called *bar lines* and they separate the music into *measures* or *bars*. Every measure contains the same number of beats.

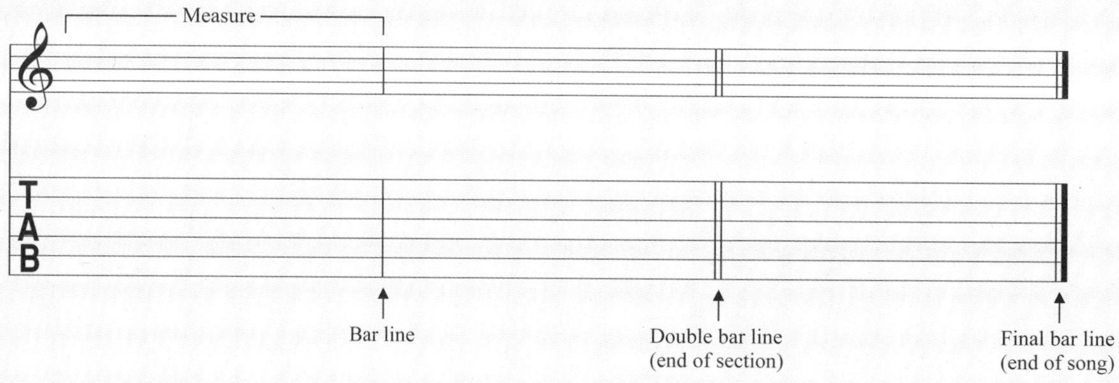

We can further divide the notes to get a note that lasts for only one beat. These notes are called *quarter notes*, and we can fit four of them into a measure when we use a 4/4 time signature. The stack of numbers you see at the start of a piece of music is called the *time signature*, and a 4/4 time signature, like the one we've been seeing so far, tells us that every measure will contain four beats.

EXERCISE 4

Let's try playing some quarter notes now, again counting along, 1-2-3-4. Make sure you play all notes evenly, on the beats, using downstrokes with the pick. To play a *downstroke*, the pick moves through the string in a downward motion, towards the floor. Watch how it's done on the video.

EXERCISE 5

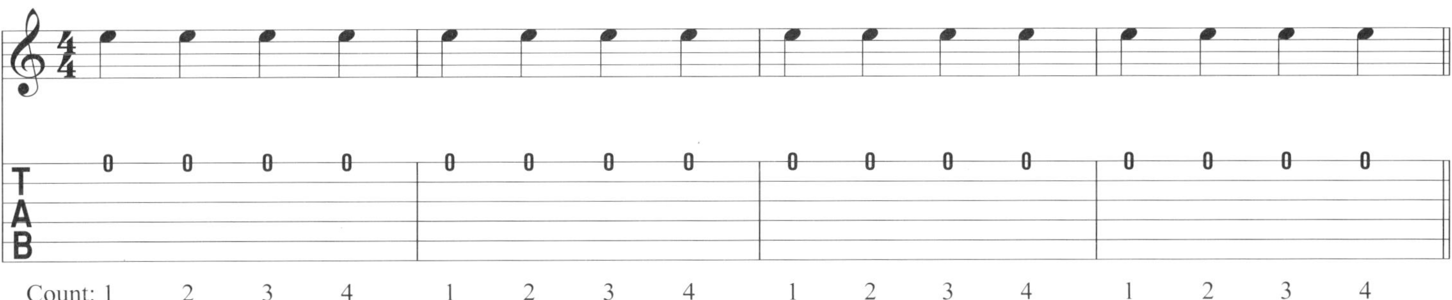

Before we learn any more note types, let's try mixing up the rhythm a bit by using quarter, half, and whole notes all in one exercise. Keep counting along, either out loud or in your head.

EXERCISE 6

Now this might have been super easy for you, or maybe it was quite difficult. If you're having any trouble playing along with the videos, spend some extra time studying and practicing the previous exercises before moving on. If you still have trouble, don't worry. We still have plenty of exercises to look at that will hone your rhythm skills, and sometimes it just takes seeing a little more of this stuff to get a hang of it.

Let's learn two more notes on the first string, the F on fret 1 and the G on fret 3.

Here are a few exercises using the notes we know so far, E, F, and G.

EXERCISE 7 

EXERCISE 8

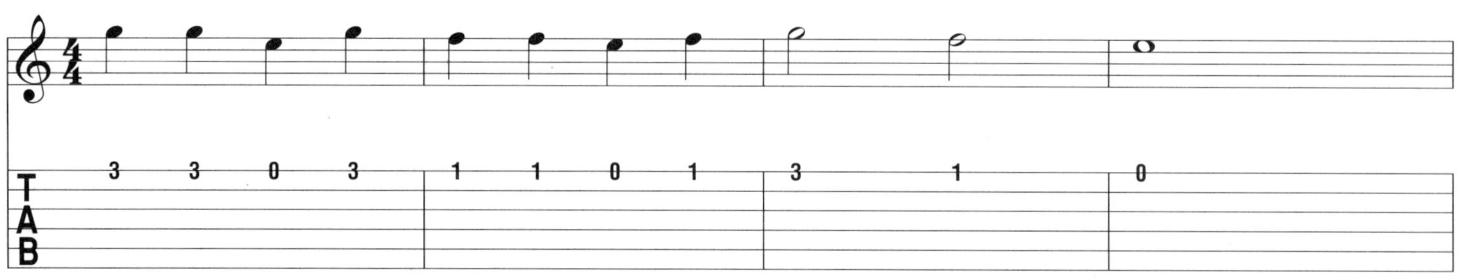

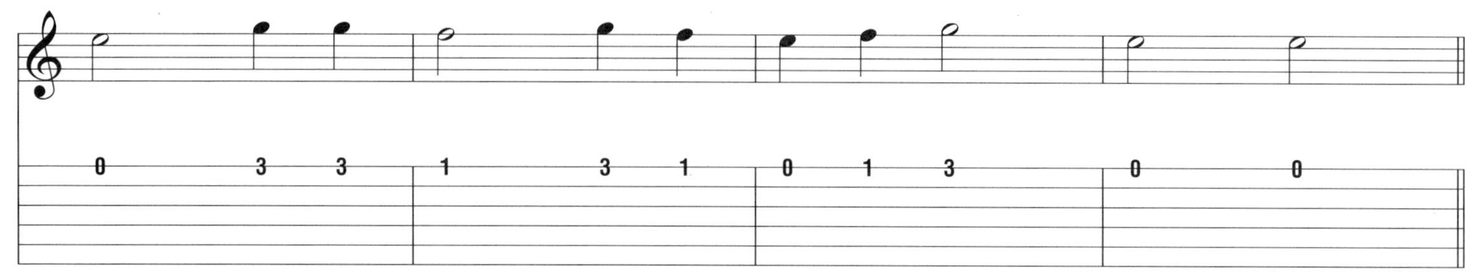

EXERCISE 9

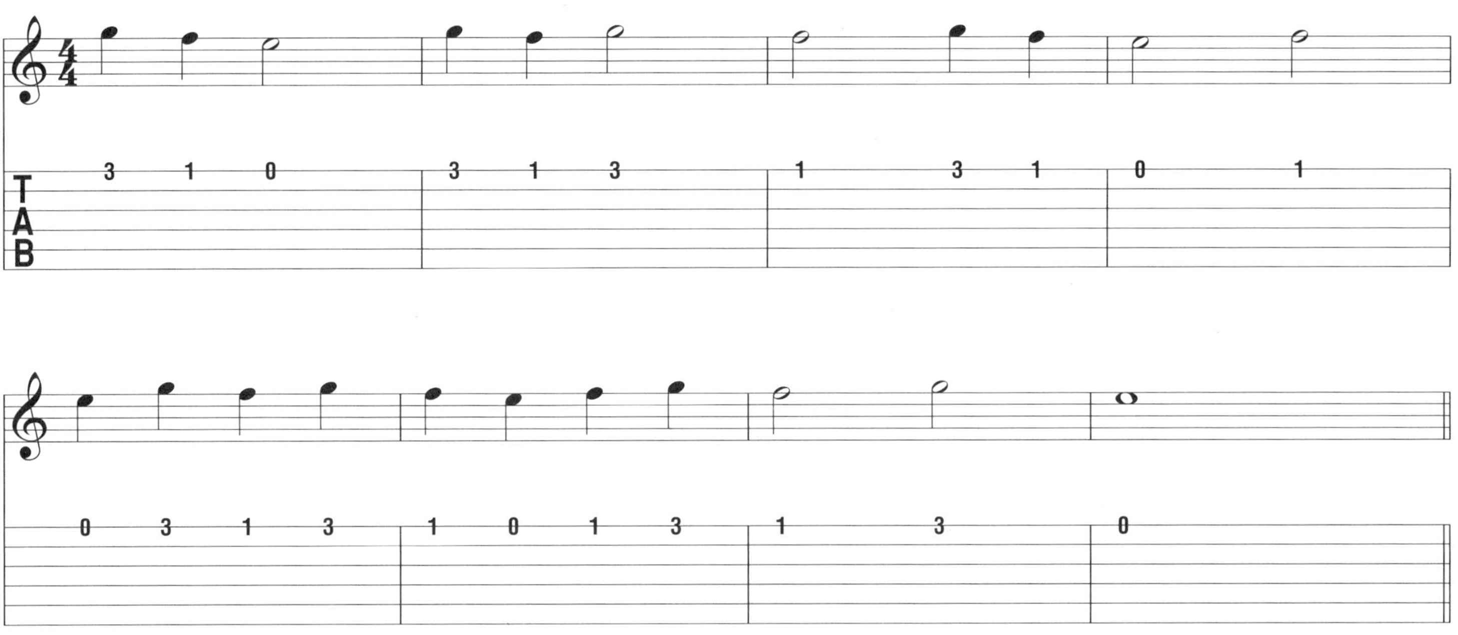

You'll want to memorize every note by both its letter name and tab number, as well as by its location in the standard notation. When playing notes, aim for touching the strings with your fingertips, and make sure you apply enough pressure. Try to keep your thumb behind the neck, even though you might see experienced players jamming out with their thumbs hanging over it. While this can sometimes work for someone who knows what they're doing, it's best to keep your thumb behind the neck when you're first starting out.

Now let's test your note-reading ability and take away the tab! Look back to where we learned these notes if you need help remembering where each note sits on the staff. The *staff* is that set of lines and spaces that we use in standard notation, and each line or space represents a different pitch.

EXERCISE 10

If you found that last exercise difficult, you'll need a little more practice reading these notes in standard notation. To get better at this, go back to some previous exercises and focus on just looking at the notes on the staff, not the numbers in the tab. While tab is very helpful and will come in handy as we learn some of the more difficult popular songs in this book, right now it's important to be able to recognize the notes both by their letter name and by where they're placed on the staff.

THE SECOND STRING

The notes we'll learn on the second string are an open B, a C at fret 1, and a D at fret 3. Again, use your first finger on fret 1 and your third finger on fret 3.

Here's an exercise using our three new notes. Remember, always think of the note names as you play them, and work on memorizing exactly where each note is placed on the staff.

EXERCISE 11

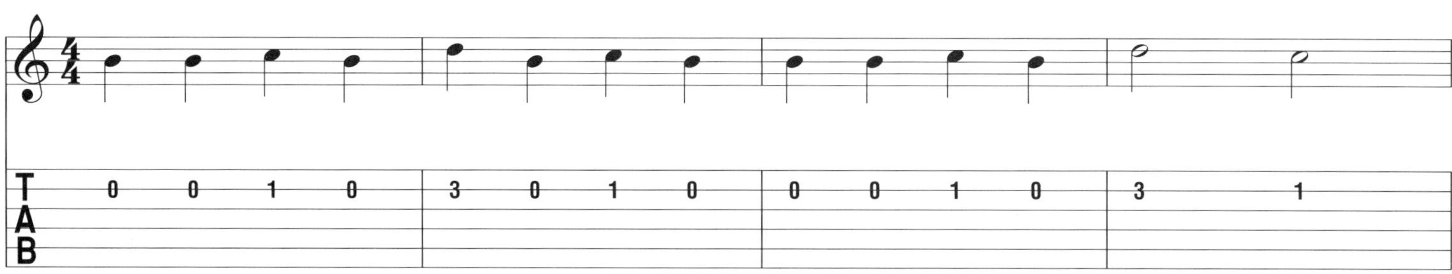

DOTTED HALF NOTES

Did you notice we learned a note that lasts for four beats (whole note), two beats (half note), and one beat (quarter note), but we don't have a note that lasts for three beats? Well, adding a dot to a half note turns it into a *dotted half note*, which is worth three beats. In fact, whenever we see a dot after a note, we always add one half the duration of the note it's attached to. So, in this case, two beats (the half note) plus one beat (the dot, or half the value of the half note) equals three beats.

Here's an exercise on the second string using the dotted half note.

EXERCISE 12

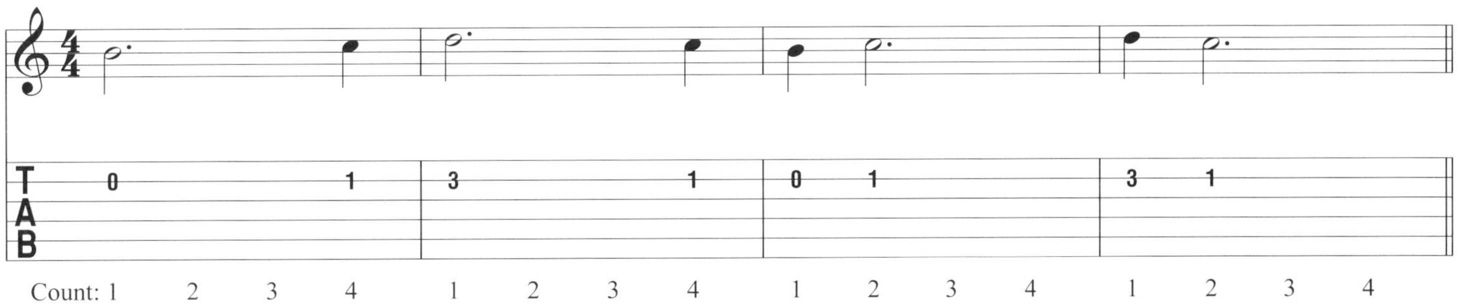

By combining notes on the first two strings, we can play our first song, "Mary Had a Little Lamb." We're going to talk about "upstrokes" soon, but for now, continue using all downstrokes with the pick.

MARY HAD A LITTLE LAMB

Traditional

THE THIRD STRING

On the third string, we get a G when we play the string open, and an A when we fret at fret 2. For the A, use your second finger.

We've now learned a G on the first and third strings, and you might be wondering how we can have two notes with the same name. The answer is that we only use the letters A through G to name notes, repeating them in order as we go higher, and this new G is simply played in a lower octave than the first G you learned. When two notes are an *octave* apart, they share the same letter name and basically sound the same, but one will sound higher or lower than the other. Play the G on the first string along with the G on the third string to hear how they sound similar.

Now that we're familiar with the notes on the first three strings, let's play some songs! Remember to count along, always lining up the notes with the beats, and try to focus on reading the notes in the standard notation instead of just looking at the tab.

TWINKLE TWINKLE LITTLE STAR

Traditional

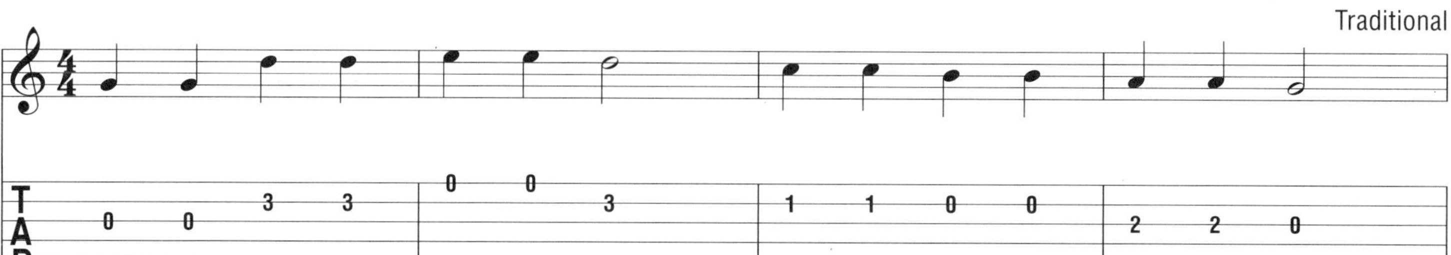

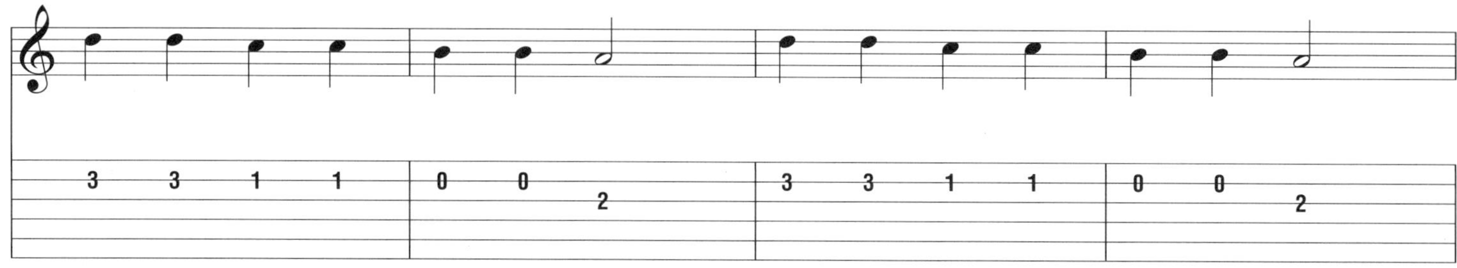

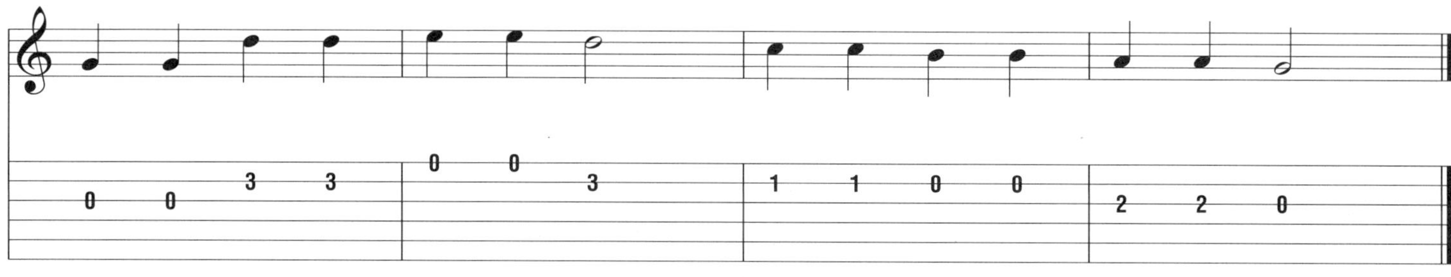

EIGHTH NOTES

Before we learn more songs, let's learn a new type of note, the eighth note. *Eighth notes* go by twice as fast as quarter notes, so you'll play two of them in the space of one quarter note. Eighth notes can be either written with a flag ♪ or connected with a beam ♫♫.

To line up eighth notes with the beat, you'll count "1-&-2-&-3-&-4-&." Using the notes we've learned on all three strings, let's try playing some eighth notes.

EXERCISE 13

DOWNSTROKES AND UPSTROKES

Up until now, we've been picking every note with a downstroke. When we need to play faster, as is often the case with eighth notes, it can be more efficient to use alternating pick strokes. In general, when using *alternate picking*, we use downstrokes ⊓ on the *downbeats* (the 1-2-3-4s) and upstrokes V on the *upbeats* (the "ands" when we count eighth notes). An *upstroke* is just the opposite of a downstroke, so you'll pick upwards through the string, towards the ceiling.

Try the previous exercise again, this time using alternate picking.

EXERCISE 14

Here's an exercise that mixes up the eighth notes with some quarter notes. Be sure to pay attention to the picking pattern!

EXERCISE 15

DOTTED QUARTER NOTES

Just like adding a dot made the half note longer, we can also make a quarter note longer by adding a dot. In this case, we'd get a *dotted quarter note*, which is worth one and a half beats. (You can also think of it as being worth three eighth notes.) This is actually much easier to hear than it is to think about. Your ear is used to hearing these rhythms, but it's harder to visualize the same rhythms on the page. Let's try using the dotted quarter note in the popular melody, "Jingle Bells." Be sure to use the indicated picking pattern. The goal here is to always play on the downbeats with downstrokes, and on the upbeats with upstrokes. (This alternation will become even more important once we start strumming chords.) Again, play along with the video to make sure you're using the correct notes and rhythms.

JINGLE BELLS

Traditional

Count: 1 & 2 & 3 & 4 &

Here's another popular melody that uses dotted quarter notes. This time, we'll take away the tab to make sure you are reading and learning the notes. While you play, don't forget to think of the actual note name, not just the tab number and where it is on the guitar.

ODE TO JOY

Ludwig van Beethoven

If you had trouble recognizing the notes without the help of the tab, go back to some previous exercises and practice playing them by only reading the notes.

NEW SYMBOLS & SIGNS

Sometimes instead of writing out a section of music again, we use *repeat signs*. When you see repeat signs, simply repeat the section that's enclosed within them once.

A *tie* is a curved line that connects two notes of the same pitch. We pick only the first note and let it sustain for the combined value of the two tied notes, as if they were one.

Rests are simply timed moments of silence. Each rest matches the same time as its similarly named note. Try and memorize what each rest looks like and how many beats each one receives.

Whole rest = 𝄻 (4 beats)

Half rest = 𝄼 (2 beats)

Quarter rest = 𝄽 (1 beat)

Eighth rest = 𝄾 (1/2 beat)

Now let's put everything we've learned so far to use in the final song of the chapter. Stroke symbols won't always be shown in the music from here on out, but if you remember to use downstrokes on the downbeats and upstrokes on the upbeats, you'll be good to go.

CAN YOU FEEL THE LOVE TONIGHT

from THE LION KING

Music by Elton John
Lyrics by Tim Rice

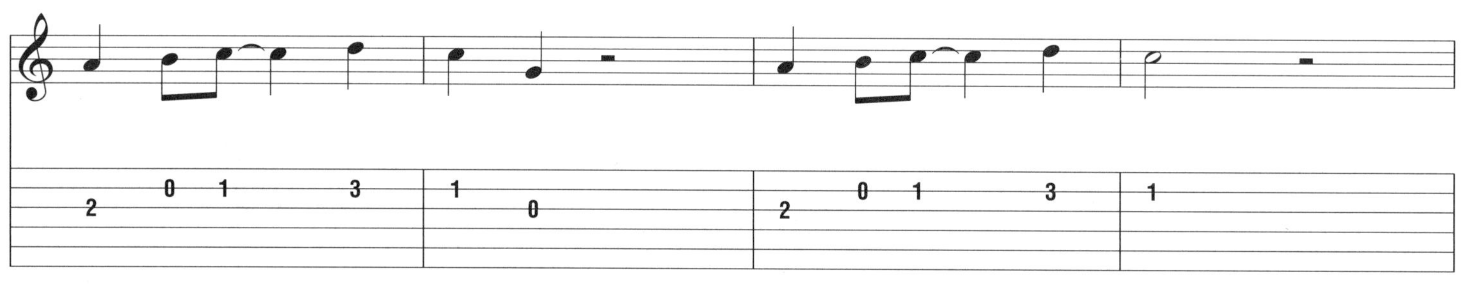

Chorus

Outro

CHAPTER 2: NOTES ON THE LOWEST THREE STRINGS

THE FOURTH STRING

The notes on the fourth string are D, E, and F. The open string is your D. You'll use your second finger on fret 2 for the E, and your third finger on fret 3 for the F.

Now let's try an exercise, without tab, using our new notes as well as some we've learned previously. To help you with the exercises in this chapter that don't include tab, here again are the notes on the first three strings.

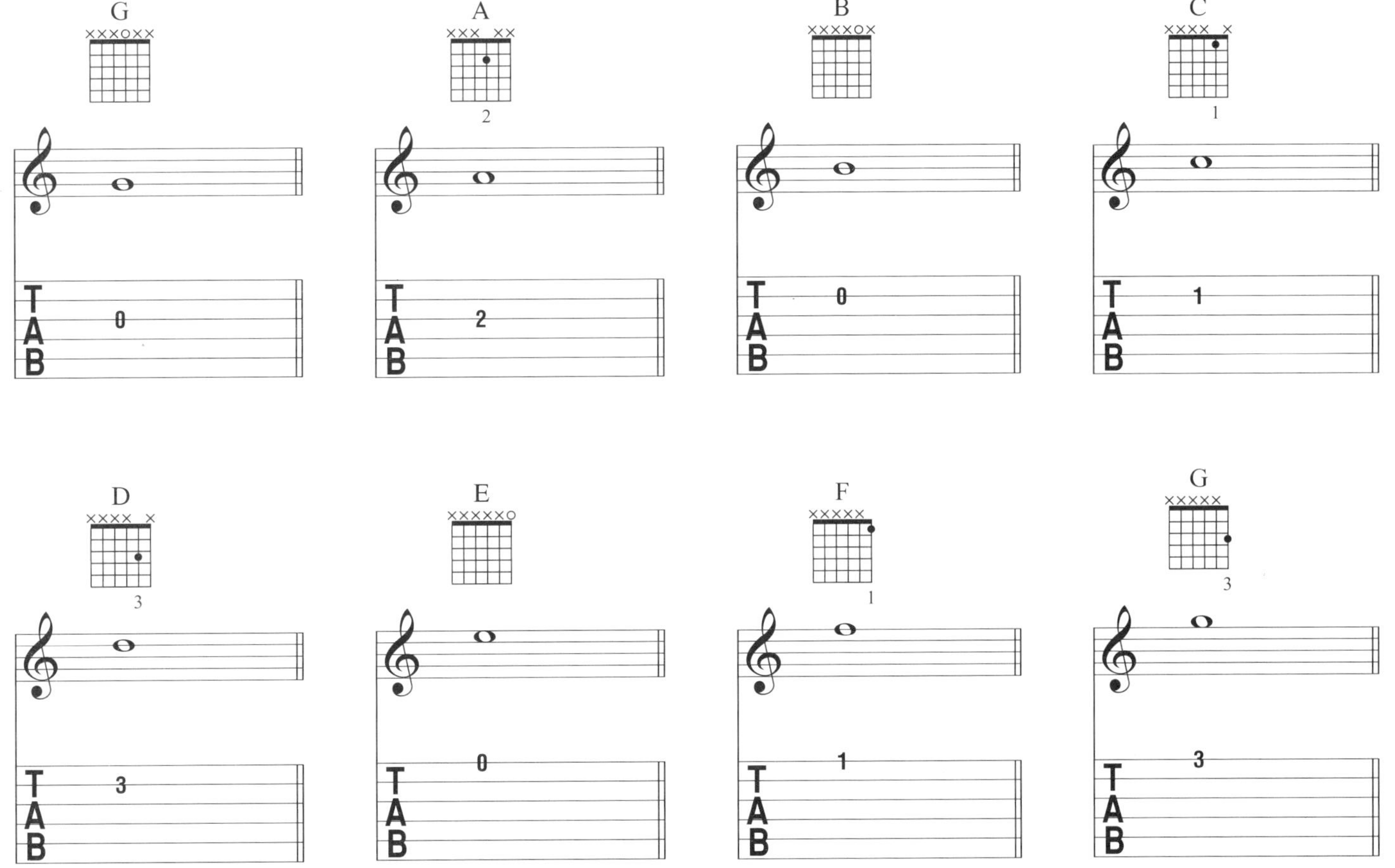

When playing through this exercise, remember to think of the note names as you play them.

EXERCISE 16

Let's try another exercise to get you used to these new notes, this time with the tab.

EXERCISE 17

```
T|----------------|----------------|----------------|----------------|
A|----3-3-1-1-----|----------------|----3-3-1-1-----|----------------|
B|------------2-2-|--------0-2-0---|------------2-2-|----------------|
 |-0-0------------|-0-0-2-3------3-|-0-0------------|-3-2-0-3-2-0-2-3|

 |----3-3-1-1-----|----3-1---------|----------------|----------------|
 |------------3-3-|--------3---1-3-|----3-3-1-1-----|----------------|
 |-0-0------------|-0-0-------2----|------------2-2-|-------------0-0|
 |----------------|----------------|-0-0------------|-0-0-2-2-3-3----|

 |----------------|----------------|----------------|----|
 |--------3-1-----|----------------|---3-1----------|----|
 |-2---2------2---|-0---0---2-0----|-------2-0------|----|
 |----------------|------------3---|-0---------3-2--|-0--|
```

THE FIFTH STRING

Now we'll learn the notes on the fifth string. The open string is A, fret 2 is B, and fret 3 is C. Notice that the fifth-string notes are placed below the musical staff on what we refer to as *ledger lines*, which are extra lines we need to add to show notes below the staff. There are also ledger lines for notes that go above the staff, and we'll see a few of these later on in the book.

Let's try an exercise now combining these new fifth-string notes with the notes from the fourth string. This one includes some trickier rhythms, so play along with the video to make sure you get them all right. Again, the goal is to use downstrokes on the downbeats and upstrokes on the upbeats.

EXERCISE 18

Now, let's take away the tab and put our note-reading to the test again. This classic melody, which you might recognize as either "Greensleeves" or the popular Christmas song "What Child Is This?," uses almost all the strings we've learned so far. Note the new 3/4 time signature. With this time signature, instead of having four beats in each measure, now we'll have three. The quarter note is still equal to one beat, just like in 4/4. The song also starts with what is referred to as a pickup measure. A *pickup measure* is an incomplete measure that leads into the first full measure of a song. So, for the pickup measure we have here, we would count the missing beats, 1 and 2, and start playing on beat 3.

GREENSLEEVES

Traditional

THE SIXTH STRING

It's time to learn the notes on our final string! On the sixth string, we'll have an open E, an F on fret 1, and a G on fret 3. All of the frets on the first string share the same note names as the frets on the sixth string, and this is because they're both E strings, just tuned two octaves apart. The notes on the sixth string can be more difficult to read, though, as they dip far below the staff on ledger lines.

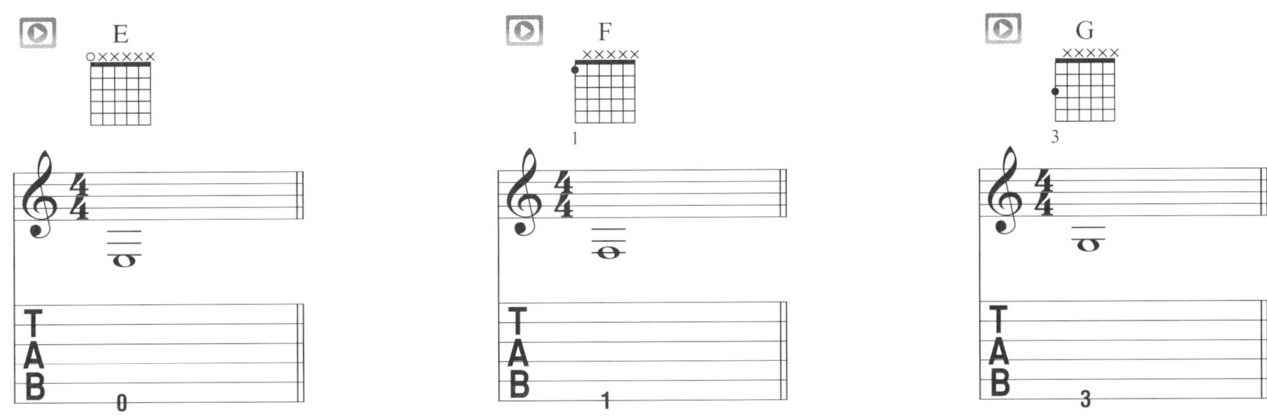

Let's see if you can recognize those new notes in the following exercise without tab.

EXERCISE 19

SHARPS AND FLATS

While we were learning the notes on the strings, did you notice that we didn't learn a note at every fret? For example, on the first string we have an F on fret 1, a G at fret 3… But what about fret 2? Well, that's where sharps and flats, known collectively as *accidentals*, come in. A *sharp* (♯) raises a note by one fret, while a *flat* (♭) lowers it by one fret. So, that note on fret 2 of the first string can be referred to as either an F♯ or a G♭. The name we choose for this note depends on what key we're in (but we'll talk a little about keys later). For now, just understand that if you see a ♯ in front of a note, play it one fret higher, and if you see a ♭ in front of a note, play it one fret lower. It's important to know that, when reading standard notation, if a sharp or flat is added to a note, that note stays sharp or flat for the rest of the measure even though the symbol isn't repeated. If we want to take an accidental off a note later in a measure, we use a *natural sign* (♮) to cancel it.

DAY TRIPPER

Words and Music by John Lennon and Paul McCartney

Did you notice anything interesting about that B in measure 6? Usually, we play that note as an open second string. But, because of the way the guitar is tuned, you'll find unison (same) notes on adjacent strings, meaning this open B can also be played on fret 4 of the third string. In the case of "Day Tripper," playing the note there just happened to fit the fingering pattern better. The unison note for every other string will be found on its adjacent lower string at fret 5. This information is handy, because what would you do if you saw a "♭" on the open B? You can't play an open string any lower, so you need to know where the B is on the third string (fret 4) and then play it one fret lower to get a B♭ (fret 3).

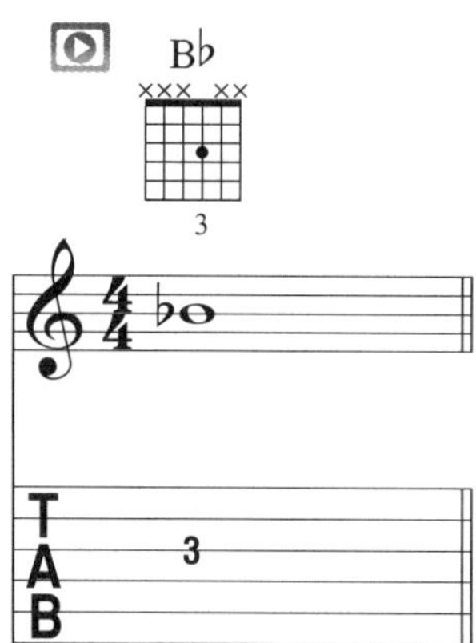

Let's try using our new B♭ note in the movie-theme classic, "He's a Pirate." You'll also see a C# near the end, but don't let that throw you off. Using what we now know about sharps, we can see that this C# is simply a C that's been moved up one fret. At the end of the song, you'll see two measures under a bracket and the number "1," called the *first ending*, and a few measures under an incomplete bracket and the number "2," called the *second ending*. This tells us that when we play through the piece the first time, we play the measures under the first ending. Then, we follow the backwards-facing repeat sign back to the forward-facing repeat sign and start playing from there again. However, the second time through we skip the first ending completely and instead play the second ending to close out the song.

HE'S A PIRATE

from PIRATES OF THE CARIBBEAN: THE CURSE OF THE BLACK PEARL

Written by Hans Zimmer,
Klaus Badelt, and Geoff Zanelli

MOVING UP THE NECK

As we discussed earlier, you can find the same note on different strings on the guitar. This is one of the things that makes learning to read notes on the guitar a little more difficult, and it's also a big reason why guitar tab can be helpful. Since tab shows you exactly which fret and string to play, it takes the guesswork out of deciding where to play a note on the fretboard. Check out this next exercise, using the classic rock riff from "Sunshine of Your Love," where we'll play the same notes in a few different positions. After that, we'll play through more of the song using just one position.

EXERCISE 20

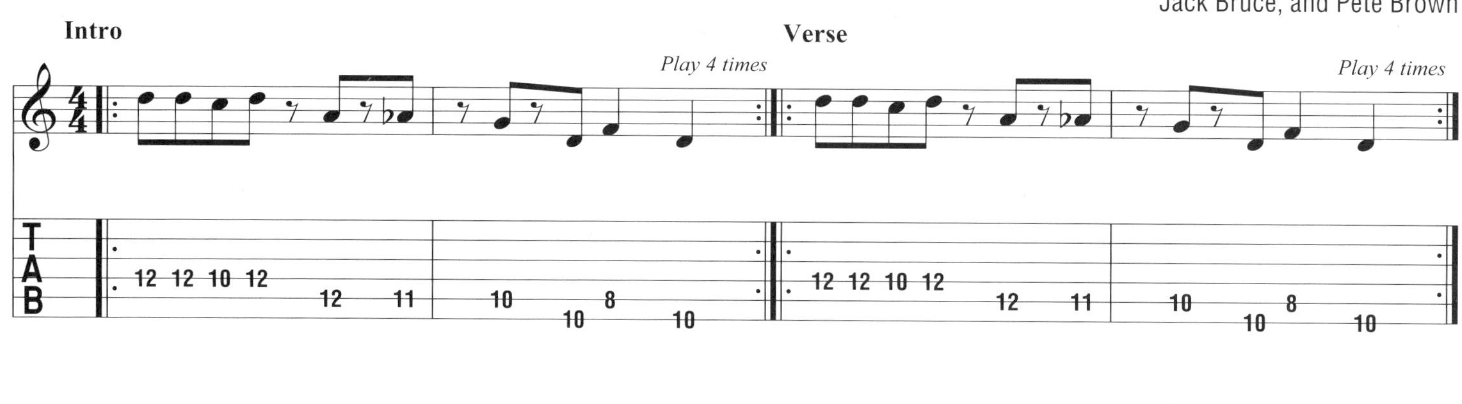

SUNSHINE OF YOUR LOVE

Words and Music by Eric Clapton,
Jack Bruce, and Pete Brown

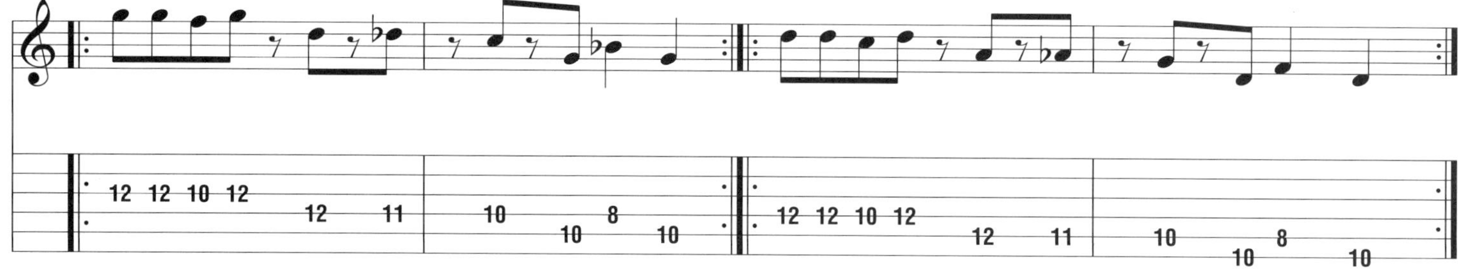

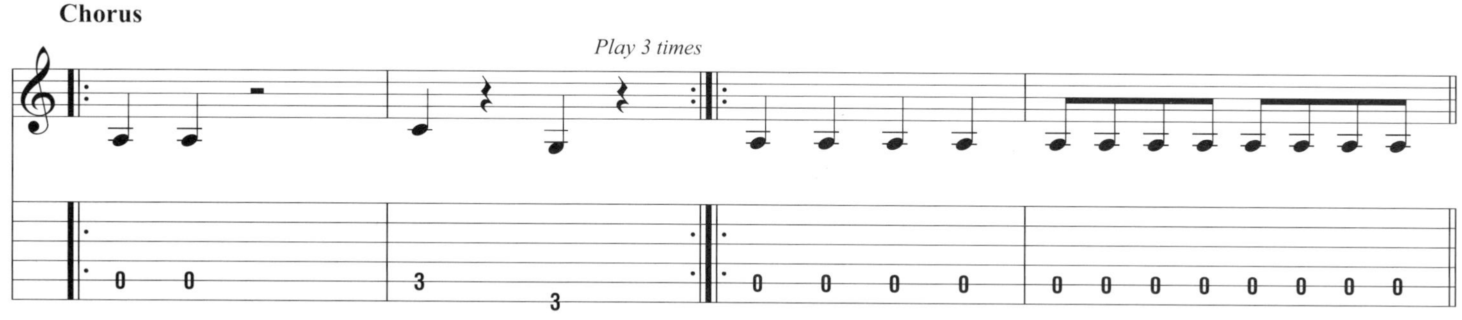

In exercise 20, we played the "Sunshine of Your Love" riff in three different positions, but we used the same notes in each. Did you notice that even though the notes were the same, the tone (or timbre) was different depending on where you played it? That's because the different string gauges (thicknesses) have an effect on the tone quality of the note, and this is often taken into account when a player decides where to play certain notes. The other factor that comes into play is the range of notes the guitarist wants to play: It's easier to stay in one position than it is to move around the neck, and while some position changes are unavoidable (or desirable), in most cases it's best to arrange a song so that you don't have to move up and down the fretboard too much.

TRIPLETS

A *triplet* is an evenly spaced three-note pattern played within the same amount of time normally filled by two notes of the same value. For example, a quarter-note triplet is three evenly spaced notes that take up the same amount of time as two quarter notes. Eighth-note triplets follow the same pattern, with three notes taking the place of two eighth notes (or one quarter note). Triplet rhythms are easier to hear than they are to read and decipher, so be sure to watch the video for the next exercise to get a handle on them. With triplets, the picking pattern can be tricky since its three-note pattern offsets the even down-up pattern we normally use. There is no rule for picking triplets, but when playing consecutive triplets, as we'll be doing in the next exercise, you can try a couple of things. Some players prefer to play each triplet with a down-up-down pattern, creating repeated downstrokes at the start of each triplet. Other players prefer to just use an alternating down-up pattern and then try and get back on track once the triplets end. (Many times, if the triplets are slow enough, you can use all downstrokes.) Either way, experiment and see what you prefer.

EXERCISE 21

Now let's take everything we've learned and put it all to use in the final song of the chapter, the iconic "Seven Nation Army" by the White Stripes. Notice the position changes, even though we play the same notes, making use of the different tones on the guitar.

SEVEN NATION ARMY

Words and Music by Jack White

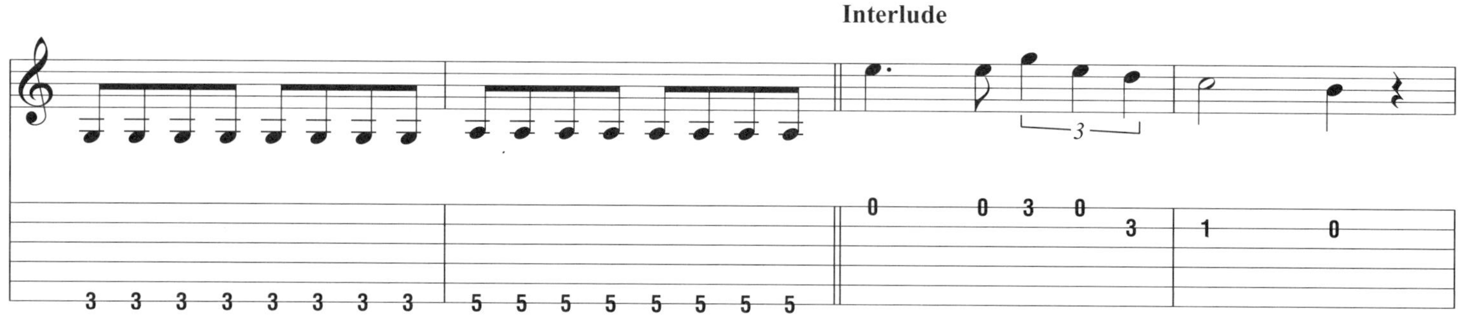

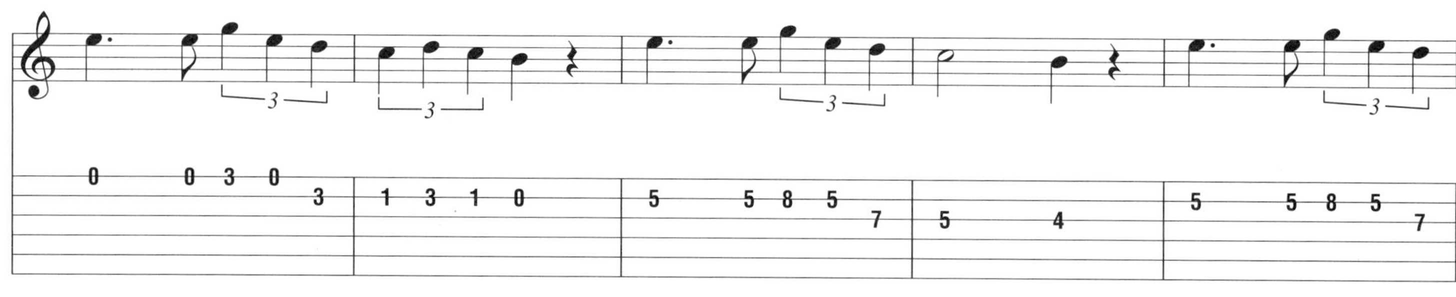

Verse

Guitar Solo

Verse

Outro

CHAPTER 3: POWER CHORDS

A *power chord* is made up of two notes, the root note and the fifth scale degree. It's not important right now to understand the music theory behind their makeup, but that's where the "5" in their name comes from. They're widely used in all styles of music and often sound great with a bit of "gain" or "distortion." So if you're playing electric, use a distortion pedal, adjust the built-in effects on your amp if it has the option, or try a digital modeler or app to get some of that "crunchy" sound.

Let's take a look at our first power chords. To strum these chords, make one downward motion with the pick, being sure to miss the unused strings. While the B5 might be a bit of a stretch at first, your fingers will eventually loosen up.

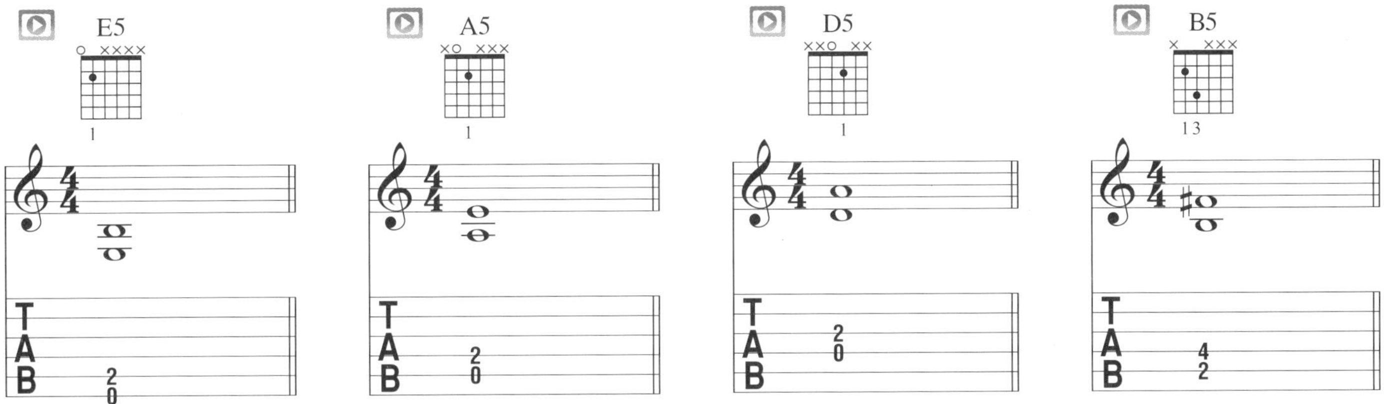

Let's try a quick exercise featuring our new E5 chord. Use all downstrokes, even for the eighth notes. Be careful not to hit the fourth through first strings. In fact, it can be helpful to play with an angled first finger that lightly touches a few of the other strings to mute them out in case you do hit them.

EXERCISE 22

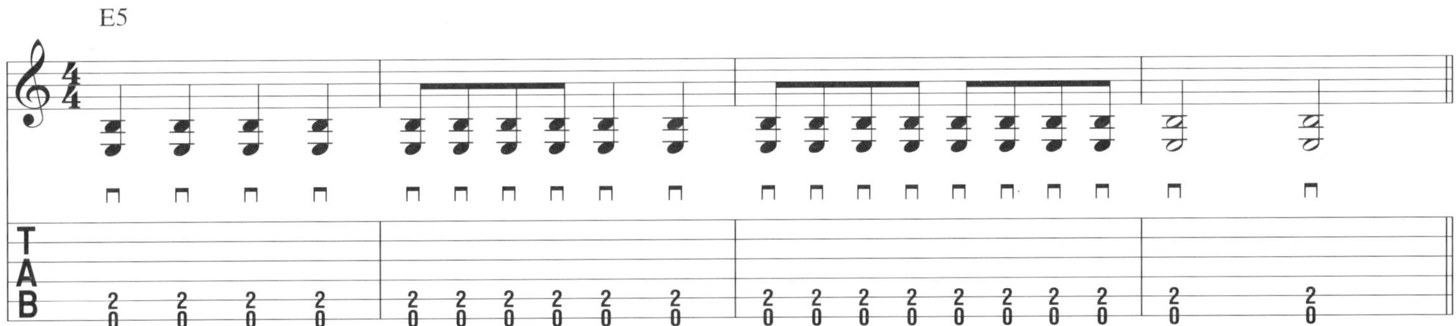

Here's an exercise that switches between the E5, A5, and D5 power chords. It's easy in the left hand, as you only have to move your first finger, but be careful with the right-hand strumming and make sure you're hearing only the correct notes.

EXERCISE 23

Let's put all of these new chords to use in the AC/DC classic, "Back in Black." The new G5/D chord is basically a power chord that's been flipped around, with the root on the top and the fifth on the bottom. We think of this chord as being *inverted*, and we'll take the different structure into account by calling it a G5/D chord (pronounced "G5 over D"). This type of chord is called a "slash chord," and we use them when a different note than usual is used as the lowest note in the chord.

BACK IN BLACK

Words and Music by Angus Young, Malcolm Young, and Brian Johnson

Chorus

A5
E5
B5
A5
B5
A5
E5
B5
A5
B5

G5/D
D5
A5
G5/D
A5
G5/D
D5
A5
G5/D
A5

A5
E5
B5
A5
B5
A5
E5
B5
A5
B5

G5/D
D5

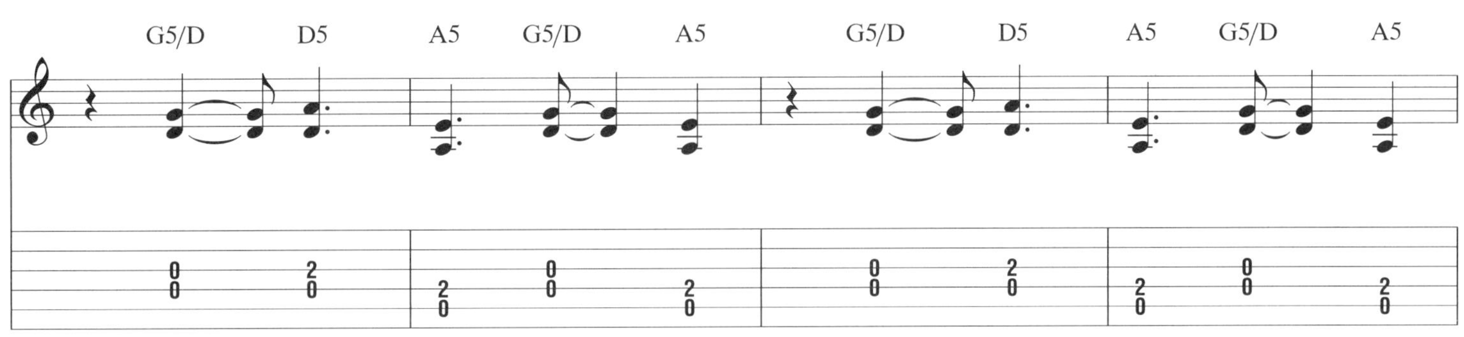

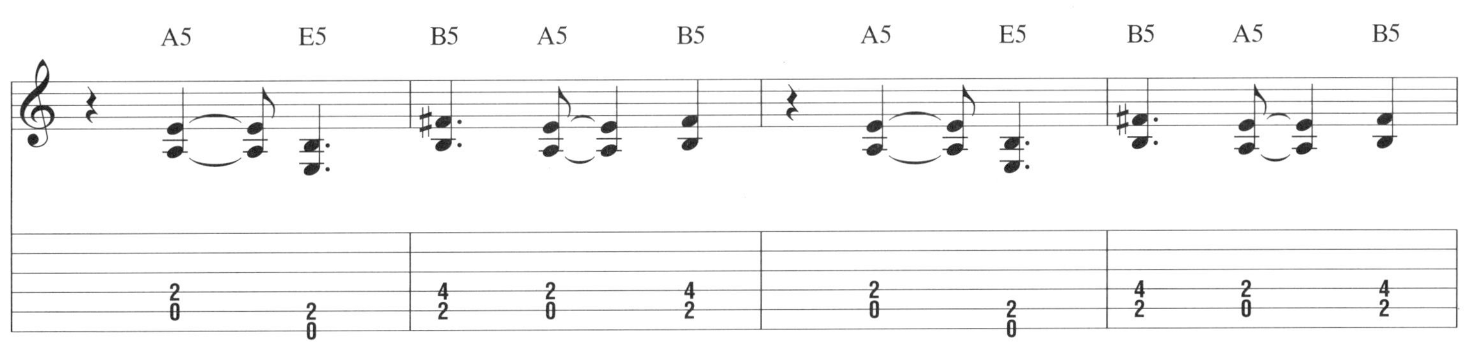

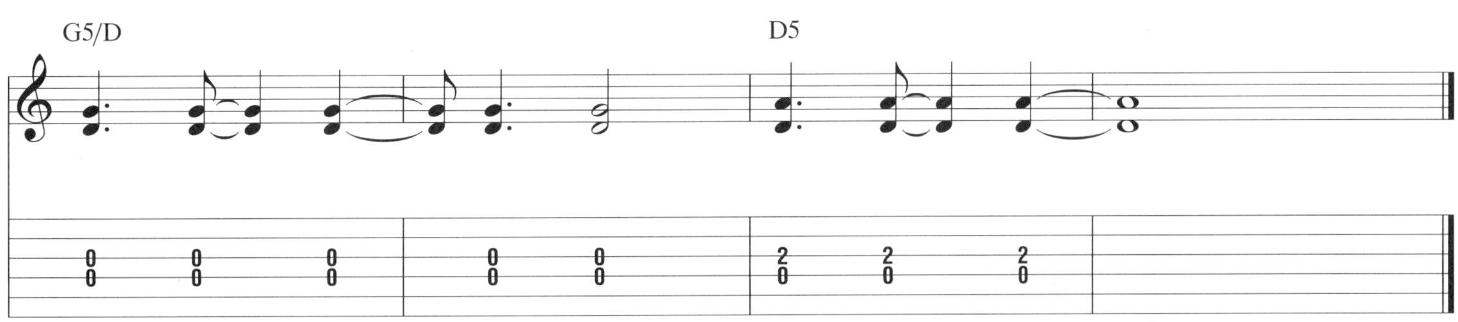

PALM MUTING

Palm muting is a popular technique that's used a lot by guitarists, especially when we play power chords. To do it, you take the fleshy pad of the right hand (on the pinky side) and rest it against the strings where they meet the saddle(s). Then, while keeping pressure there, you pick the notes, producing a slightly muted sound. If you rest too much of your right hand on the strings, you won't hear any pitch. If you're too far off the other way, towards the bridge, you won't get enough of the palm-muted sound.

We'll try using palm muting in the upcoming exercise. It will take some experimentation and time to get comfortable with this new technique, so watch the video and listen closely to make sure you're doing it correctly. Pay attention to how the measures alternate between palm muting and no palm muting, and listen closely to hear the difference. In music, palm muting is notated with "P.M." along with a dashed line to tell you how long to do it. In this exercise, we'll use a G5 power chord, which uses the same general shape as the B5—in fact, all power chords use this same shape!

EXERCISE 24

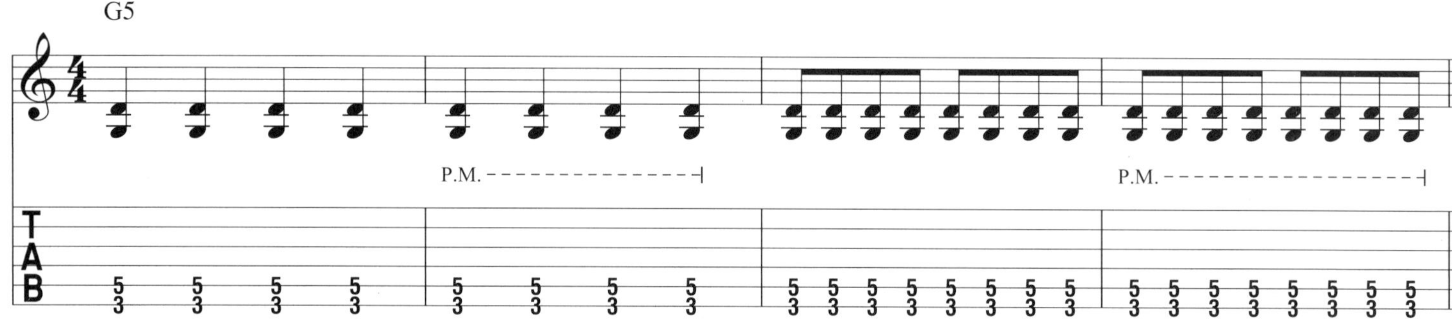

Learning new power chords will now simply be a matter of moving that shape around the neck to different positions on different sets of strings. You'll want to start thinking about and remembering these chords by their name, instead of just relying on the tab. Let's try another tune that uses numerous power chords, Adele's "Rolling in the Deep." Notice how, when we play the pre-chorus, we don't use palm muting on the first beat, but we do pick up palm muting for the rest of the measure. For the chorus, we're not using any palm muting at all. In this song, the palm-muting technique builds one dynamic in the verse and another in the chorus, helping to separate the sections.

ROLLING IN THE DEEP

Words and Music by Adele Adkins
and Paul Epworth

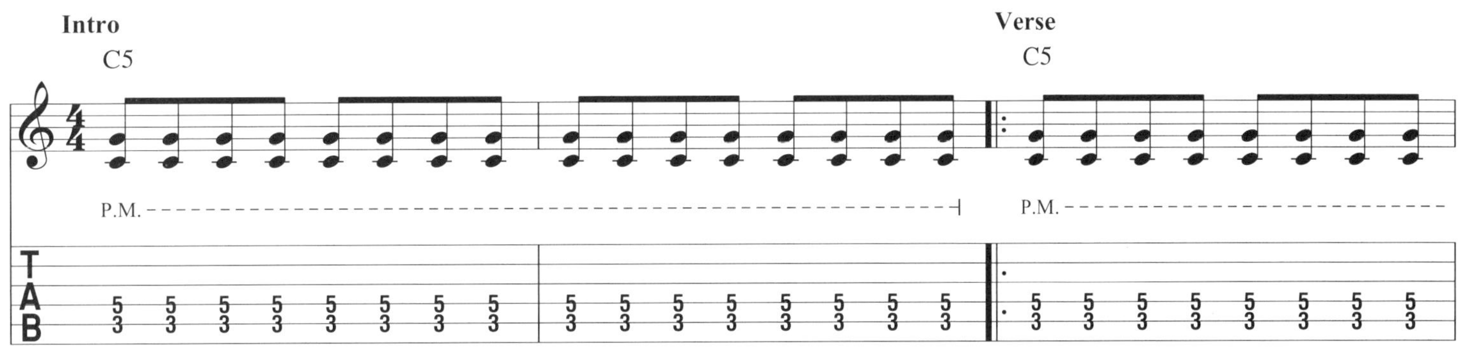

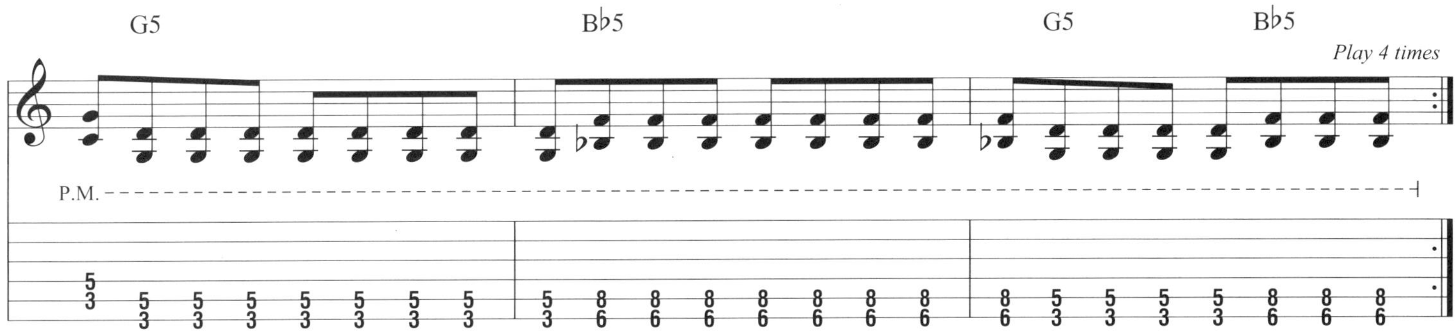

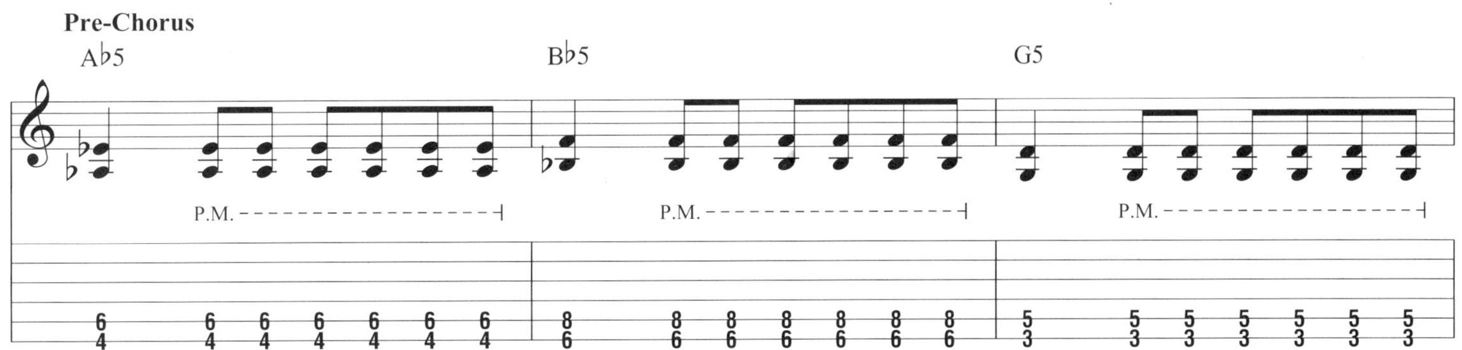

To make those power chords sound fuller, we can add one more note on top. This added note is simply the upper octave of the root note, and we fret it right underneath the third finger with the pinky. We can use this expanded shape on all power chords rooted on the sixth and fifth strings.

EXERCISE 25

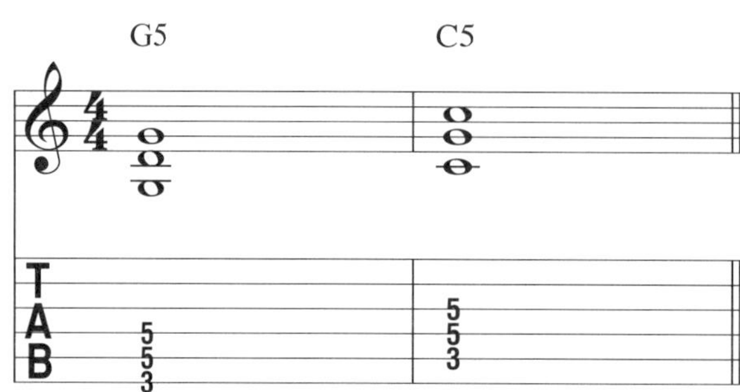

Let's put these three-note power chords to use in the smash hit from Taylor Swift, "You Belong with Me." We'll start out with our original two-note power chords in the intro and verse, using palm muting. Then we'll hold out the three-note versions for the pre-chorus, while strumming them for the chorus. Use all downstrokes for the verse but alternate your picking when you get the chorus. Since it's been a few pages since we've played single notes, the vocal and banjo melodies are also written out to provide more practice with single notes. There's no tab for the melodies, making it a good test of your note-reading ability, so go back and review your note names if you're having trouble recognizing them. Play along with the online audio, first with the melody notes and then again with the chords.

YOU BELONG WITH ME

Words and Music by Taylor Swift
and Liz Rose

A5
C5
P.M.

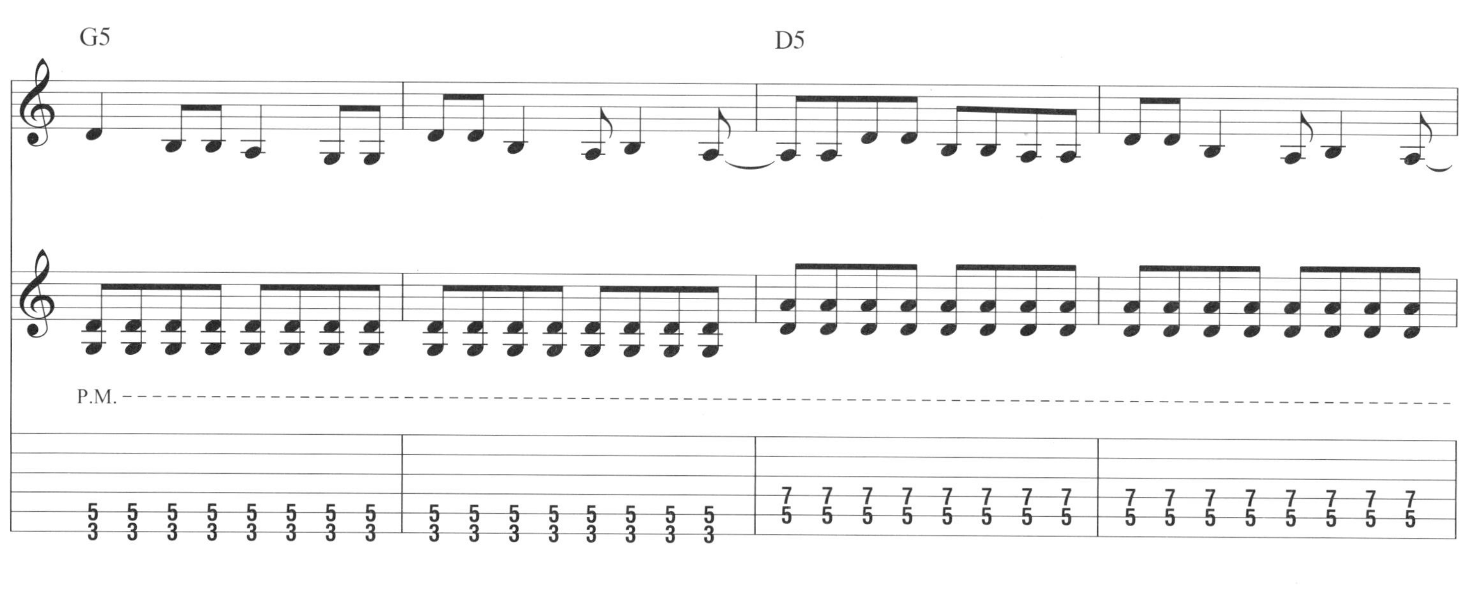
G5
D5
P.M.

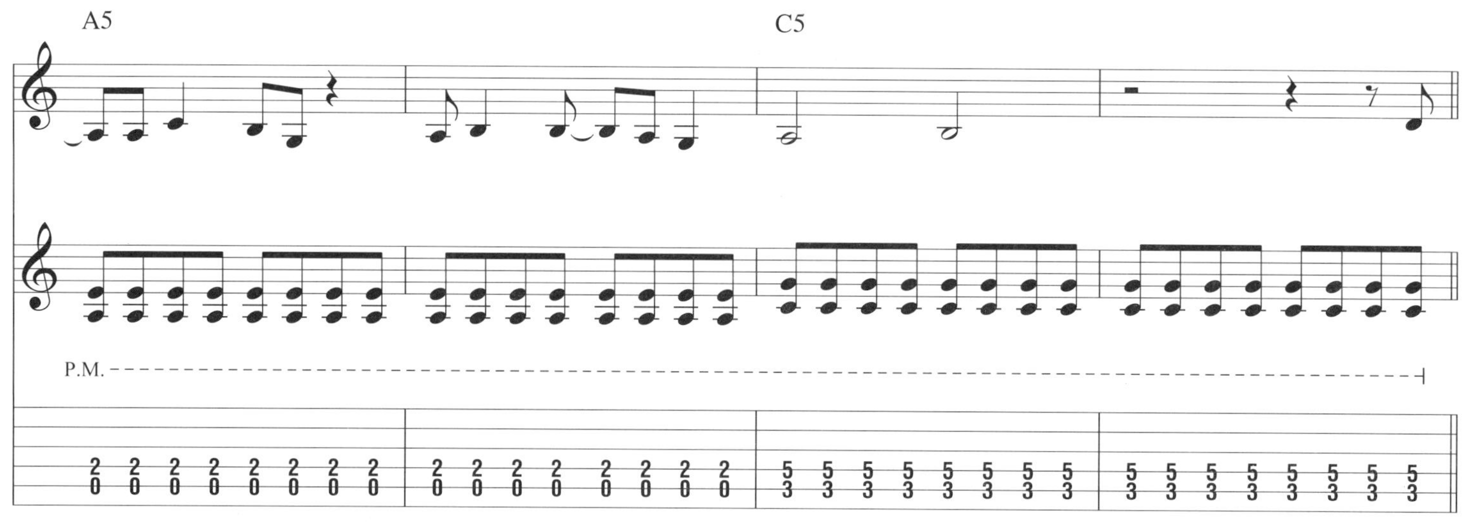
A5
C5
P.M.

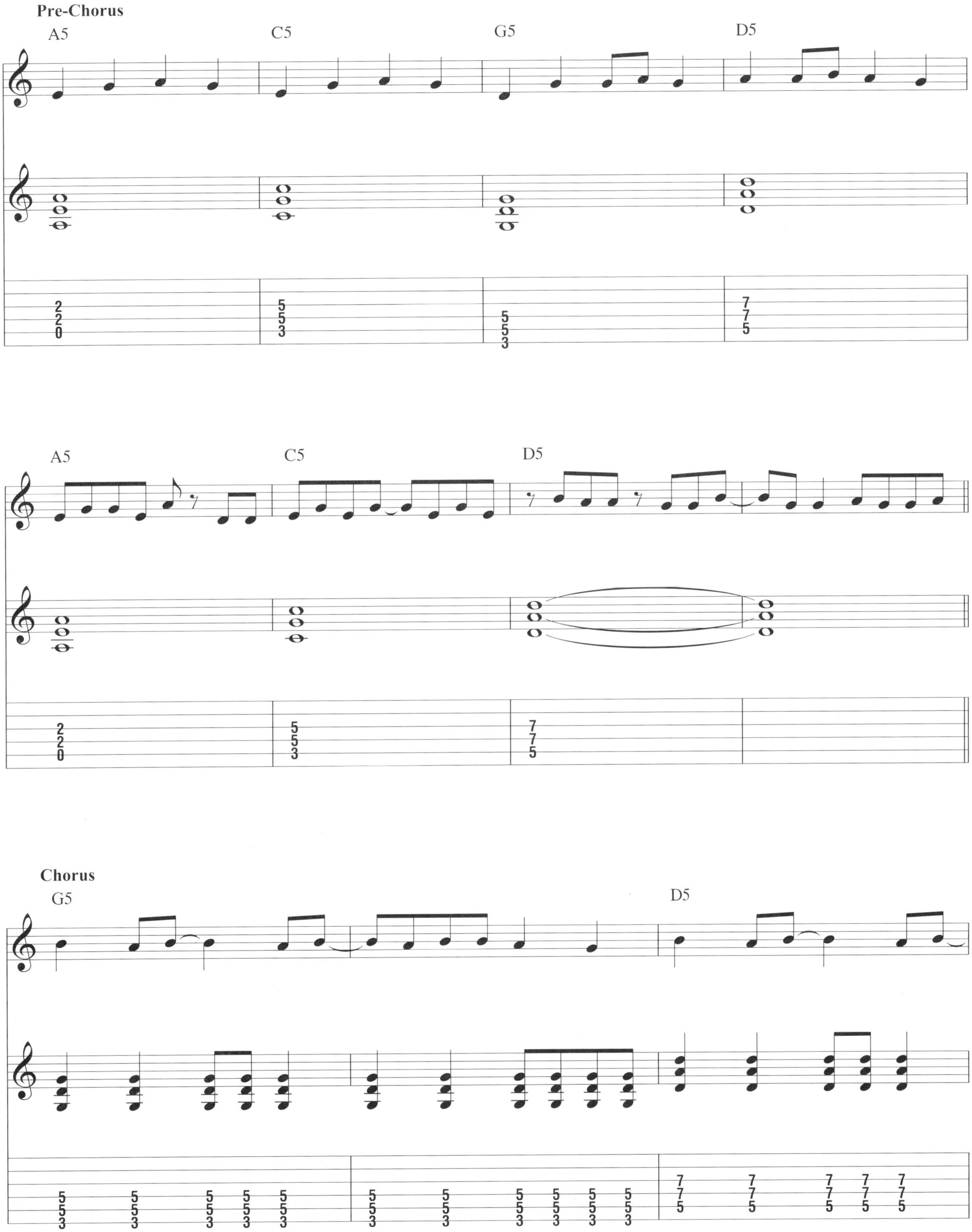
Pre-Chorus
A5
C5
G5
D5
A5
C5
D5
Chorus
G5
D5

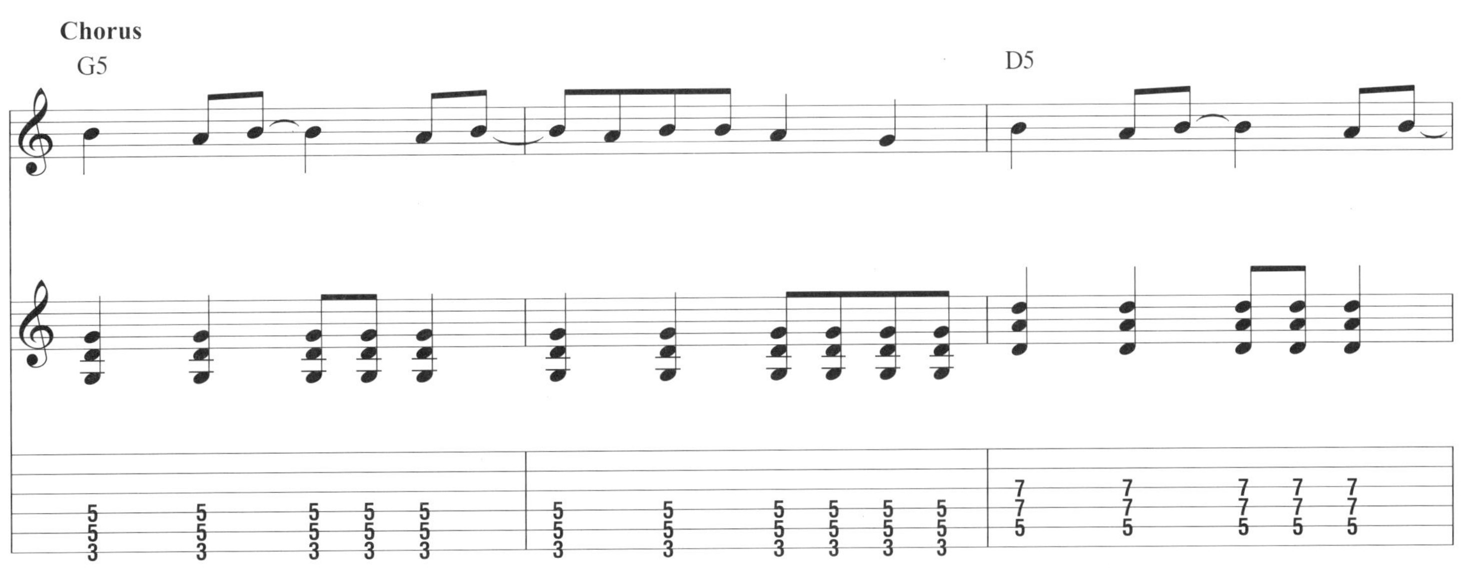

A5 C5

G5

P.M.

BARRES

For our final song of the chapter, we'll learn a new technique called barring. Simply put, a *barre* involves fretting two or more strings on the same fret with one finger. It goes against the common theme of fretting with your fingertip because to barre effectively you'll need to play with your finger flat against the fretboard. We'll start off easy with a two-string barre, but eventually we'll barre across all six strings!

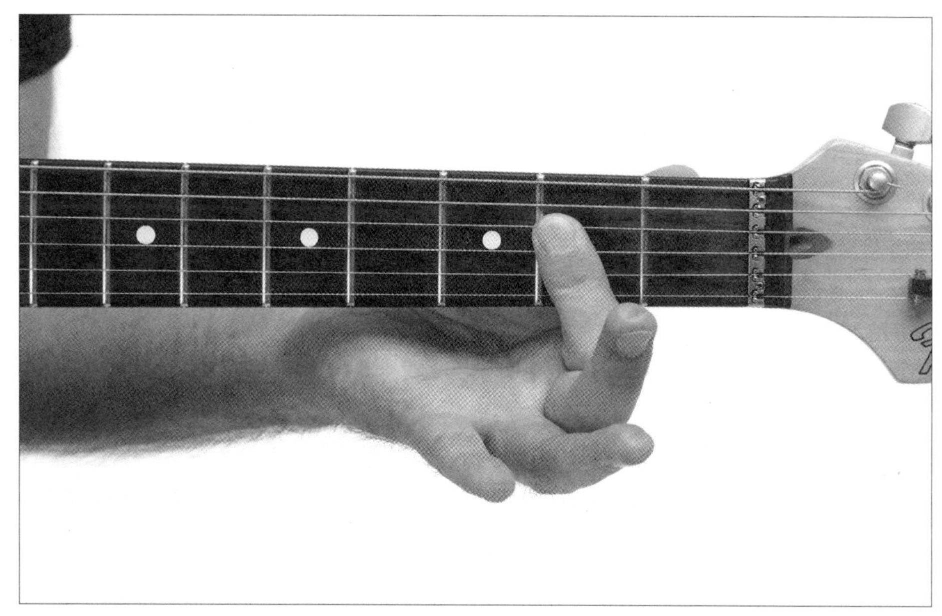

Take a look at the barres we'll use for the opening riff of our next song, "Smoke on the Water." We'll use our first finger to barre the notes on fret 3, and our third finger to barre the notes at frets 5 and 6. Check out the video to see the technique in action. When you're ready to give it a try yourself, be sure to keep your fingers straight and flat.

EXERCISE 26

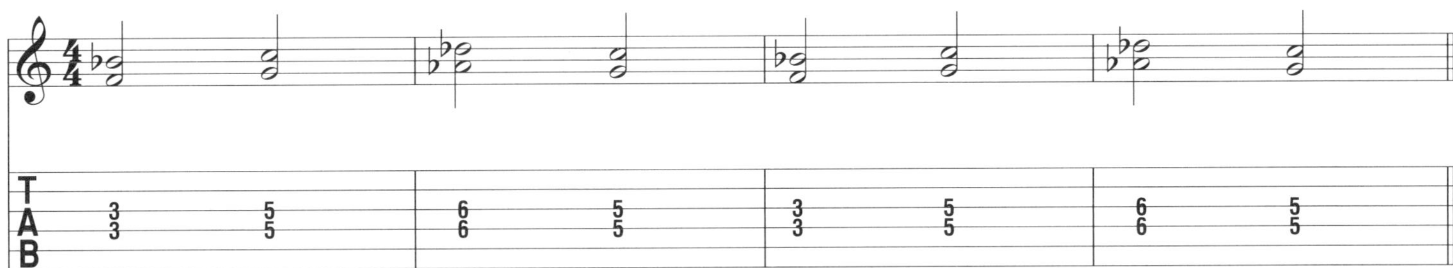

We can even use a barre to play those new three-note chords we just learned. Use your first finger for the root note, then barre with your third finger to cover the other two notes. There's no right or wrong way to finger those chords, just personal preference, so try barring all of the chords in this next exercise and see what you think.

EXERCISE 27

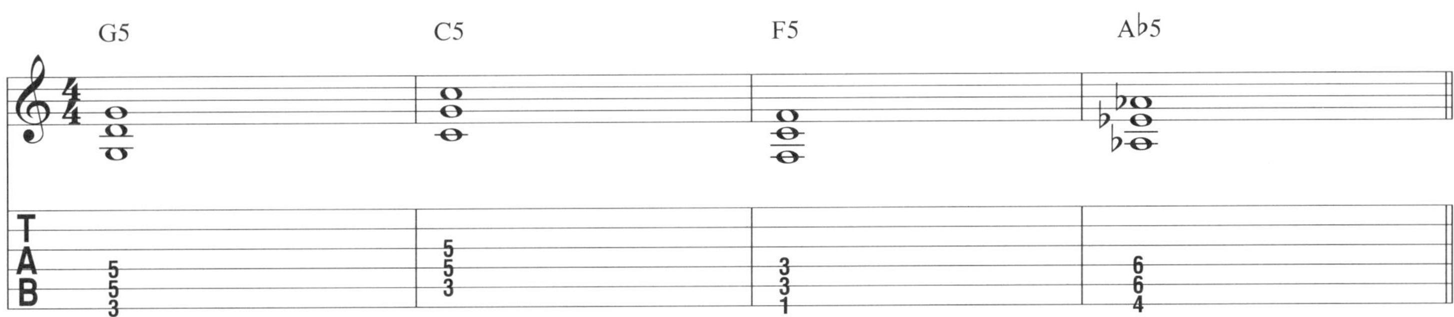

Playing power chords presents a great opportunity to learn the note names on the sixth and fifth strings, and this is because the name of each chord is based on the lowest note that you're playing on the sixth or fifth string. Knowing the note names on all six strings seems like an overwhelming task but look at it this way: If you start by using power chords, and later barre chords, to help you memorize the note names on the sixth and fifth strings, then by knowing the sixth string, you will also have learned the first string. Although the strings are two octaves apart, they share the same note names. So, right there you would now know 50 percent (three strings) of the notes on the guitar. Not bad, right? And if you're curious about the notes beyond fret 12, remember that fret 12 is on octave apart from the open string and uses the same name as the open string, so simply imagine fret 12 as the open string and envision those higher frets in relation to those notes you know on the lower frets.

CODAS

When playing a song, we sometimes need to go back and repeat a section before jumping to a separate ending. In written music, this can be done with a *coda*, a new section that ends a song, along with special directions to help us get there. "D.S. al Coda" tells us to go back to the section marked with a D.S. symbol 𝄋, play from there until we reach the "To Coda" marking, and then jump to the coda 𝄌 to finish the song. "D.S." stands for *dal segno*, an Italian term that means "from the sign," so "D.S. al Coda" is telling you to go back and play "from the sign to the coda."

Let's put everything we've learned together for our final song of the chapter, "Smoke on the Water."

SMOKE ON THE WATER

Words and Music by Ritchie Blackmore, Ian Gillan,
Roger Glover, Jon Lord, and Ian Paice

Verse
G5
P.M.
Chorus
F5
G5
Play 4 times
C5
A♭5
P.M.
To Coda
G5
C5
A♭5
Interlude
G5/D

Guitar Solo
G5
C5
G5
Play 4 times
P.M.
C5
F5
D.S. al Coda
G5/D
Coda
G5/D
Repeat and fade

CHAPTER 4: OPEN POSITION CHORDS

Open position chords are the most common type of chord played on the guitar. Generally, when you hear a guitar being strummed, those are most likely open position chords. They're played within the first four frets of the fretboard and often contain open strings. Learning a few popular open position chords will give you the tools you need to play a wide variety of songs in many musical styles.

Let's start off with a basic G chord. Strum all six strings with a downward motion.

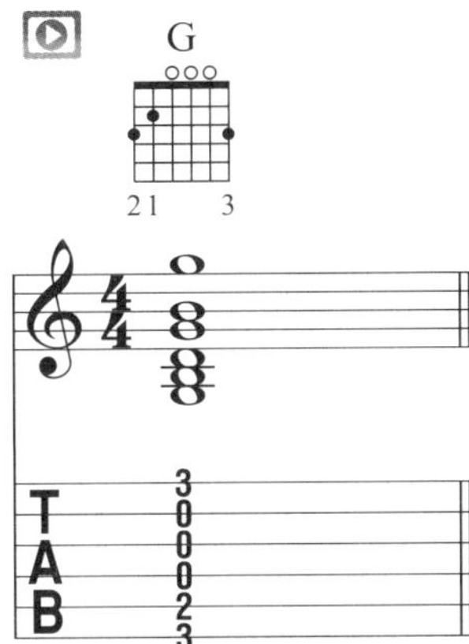

Play each note of the chord individually to make sure they're all ringing clearly. If not, one of your fingers might be blocking an open string so you'll need to adjust. It's important to get the fingers standing straight up and to fret the strings with your fingertips.

Here's another chord, C. For this C chord, we don't strum the sixth string.

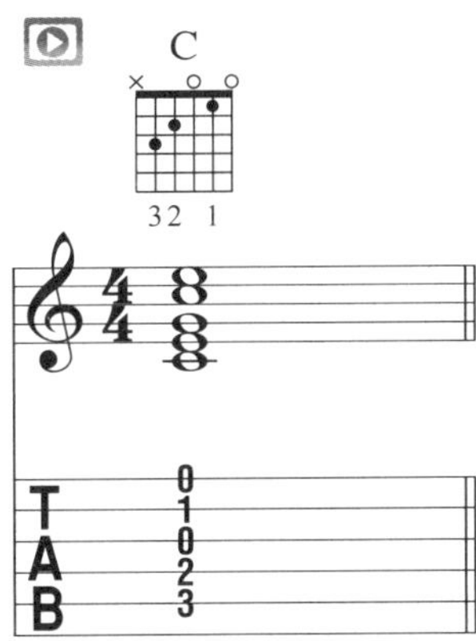

It's important to recognize these chords by their name. Most of the time, you'll just be given the chord letter without the tab or a chord chart.

Finally, let's learn the D chord. For this one, we'll only strum the top four strings, with the fourth string being left open.

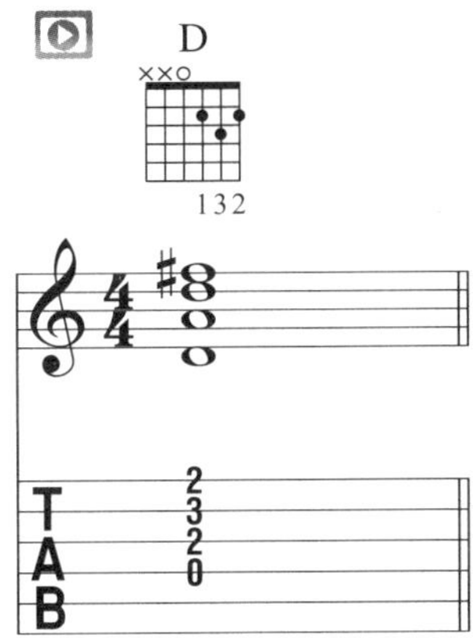

Phase one of playing these chords is just getting them to sound good. Again, play each note separately to make sure each string is ringing clearly. Phase two is a bit more challenging. It involves being able to move from chord to chord seamlessly. Since songs almost always contain more than one chord, we'll need to learn how to switch between them. And, importantly, we'll also need to play these chords in rhythm. In other words, just like when we played single notes, we want to eliminate the gaps and make smooth transitions.

Here's an exercise to get you started. Don't get discouraged if transitioning in time between chords seems difficult at first. This is a major hurdle to get over. At first, you'll be forming these chords one finger at a time, but eventually you'll be able to get all fingers in position at the same time and make quick, smooth transitions.

EXERCISE 28

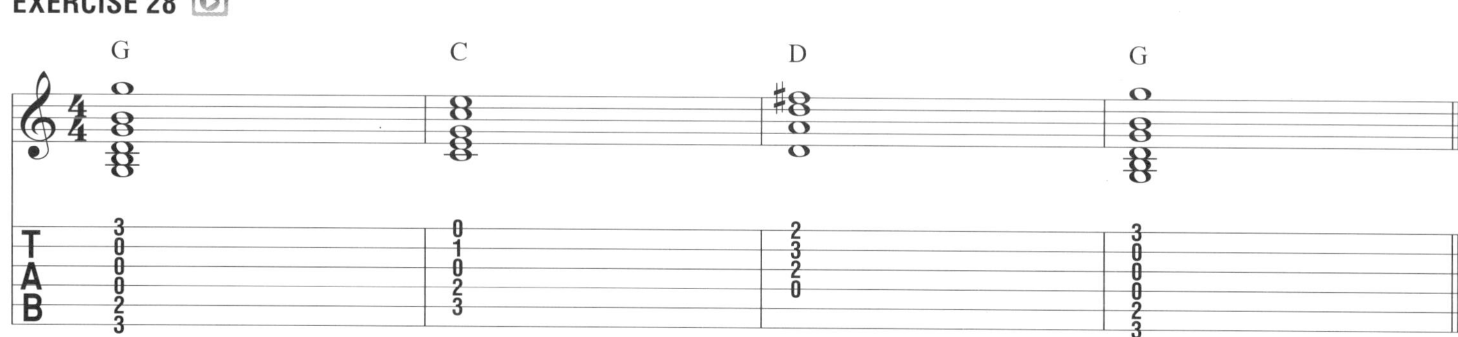

Here's one more new open position chord that you'll need to know, Em (the "m" stands for "minor"). It's the easiest of the open chords we've learned so far, so it shouldn't take much for this one to feel comfortable. We'll strum all six strings.

Notice that the suggested fingering for the Em chord was fingers 1 and 2. You could also use 2 and 3—or even 3 and 4 for that matter! Many times, with fingering choices for chords, we'll look at what chord precedes or follows. For example, if you end up playing a G chord after this Em chord, then fingers 1 and 2 work great for Em because you can leave your first finger down when moving to G (the first finger is common to both chords). Anytime we can find common notes within chord changes, it makes sense to choose fingerings that allow us to leave a finger down, as opposed to changing all the fingers.

As long as we're discussing alternative chord fingerings, let's check out a fingering variation for the G chord.

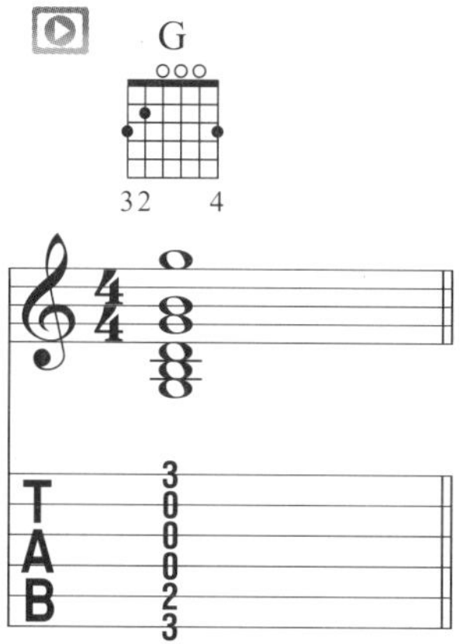

You might wonder why we'd ever think of fingering a G chord this way since that pinky stretch probably feels a bit awkward. This seemingly odd fingering starts to make sense when we have a chord pattern that moves from G to C, which many songs do, as it keeps the second and third fingers in the same general position. The fingering allows these two fingers to move as a unit from the sixth and fifth strings (for the G chord) to the fifth and fourth strings (for the C). It also leaves the first finger free and in a good spot to quickly grab the high C in the C chord. This fingering may feel more difficult at first, but stick with it. Once your fingers get used to the feeling, it will make moving between G and C much easier.

Check out the following exercise. We'll do the G the old way for the first four measures, and then we'll use the new fingering for the final four measures. Notice how much more efficient the new fingering looks when you switch between G and C. Again, it might not feel easy at first, but give it time.

EXERCISE 29

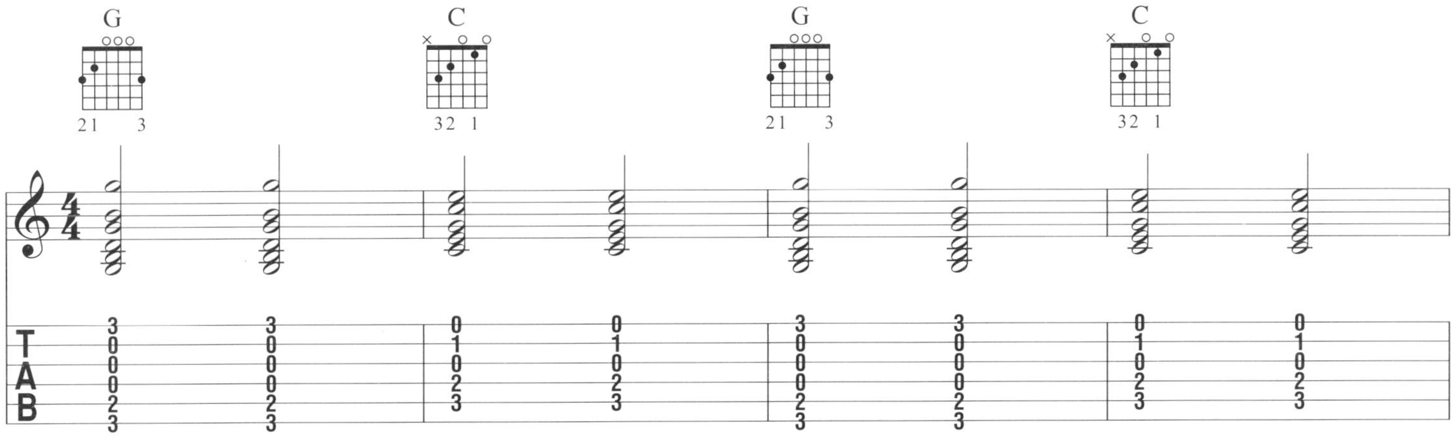

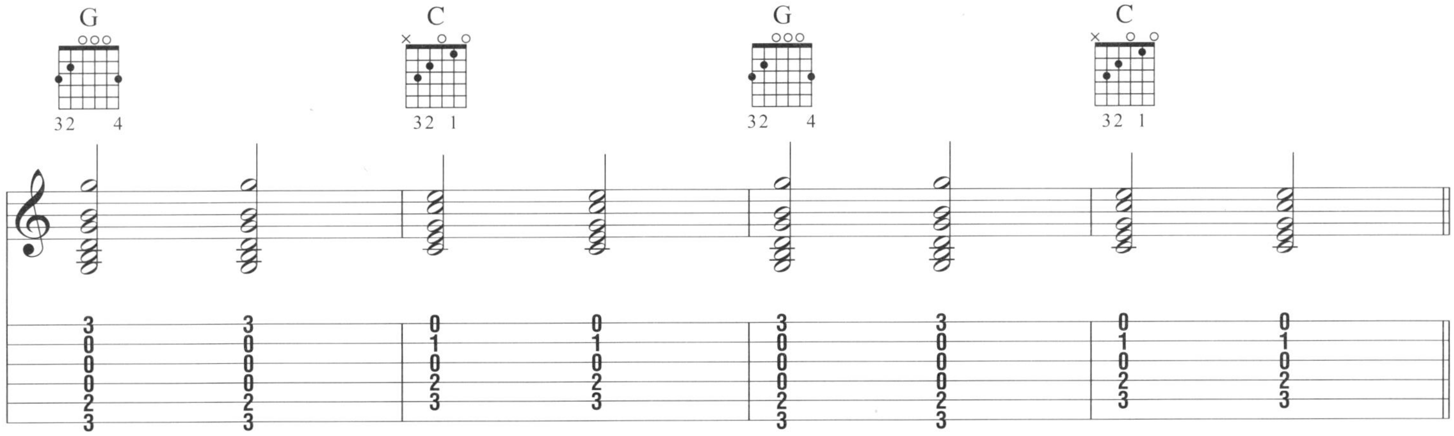

G C G C
21 3 / 32 1 / 21 3 / 32 1

G C G C
32 4 / 32 1 / 32 4 / 32 1

Now let's try all of our new open chords in a real song, the ever-classic "Brown Eyed Girl." We'll just be strumming once for each measure, giving you some time to get from one chord to the next. As soon as you play a chord, start thinking about the next chord and try to prepare your fingers for the change. Also, try some fingering variations for the Em chord to see what works best for you. Remember, if you can keep a finger down between chord changes, that is the best option.

KEY SIGNATURES

When a sharp or flat is always included on a certain note in a piece of music, we'll often show the accidental just once at the beginning in what we call a *key signature*, rather than writing it out every time we need it. Having an F# in the key signature, as we see in "Brown Eyed Girl," means that we're playing the key of G major. Every key has a different number of accidentals, and those notes will stay sharp or flat the whole time unless one includes a natural sign. While we won't cover keys and key signatures extensively in this book, it's important for you to have a basic understanding of what they're all about.

BROWN EYED GIRL

Words and Music by Van Morrison

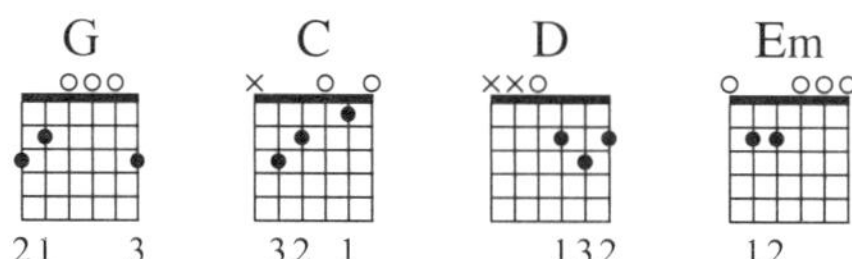

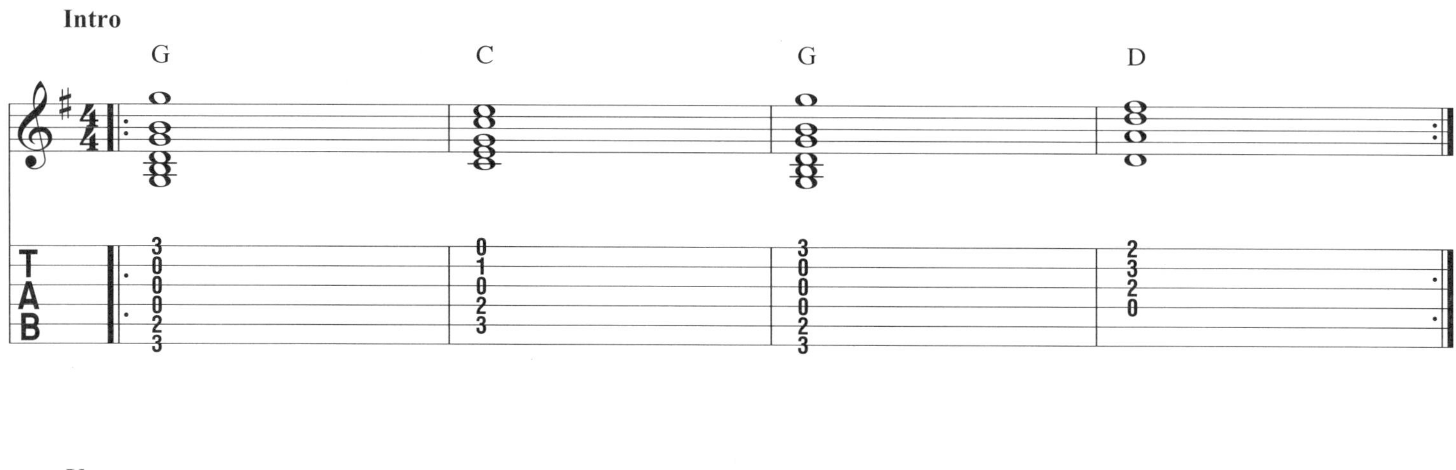

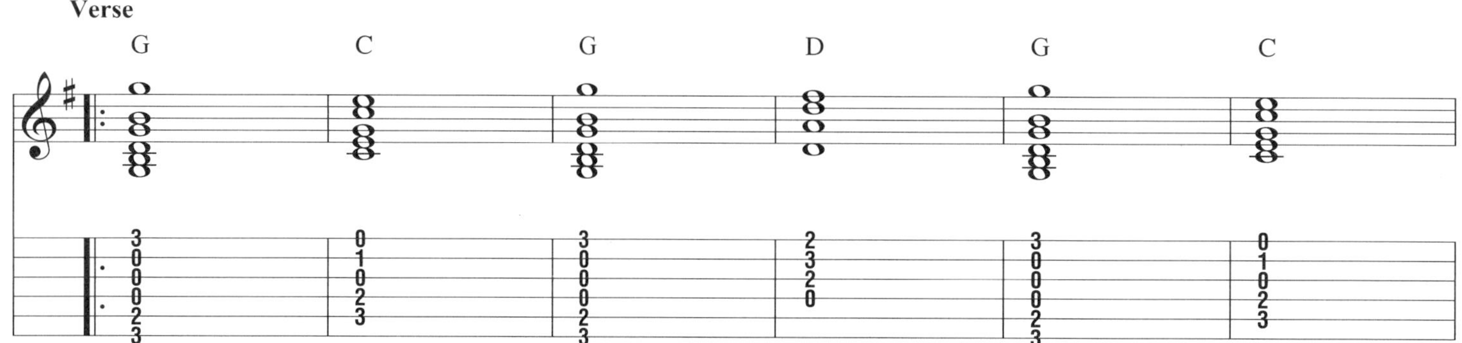

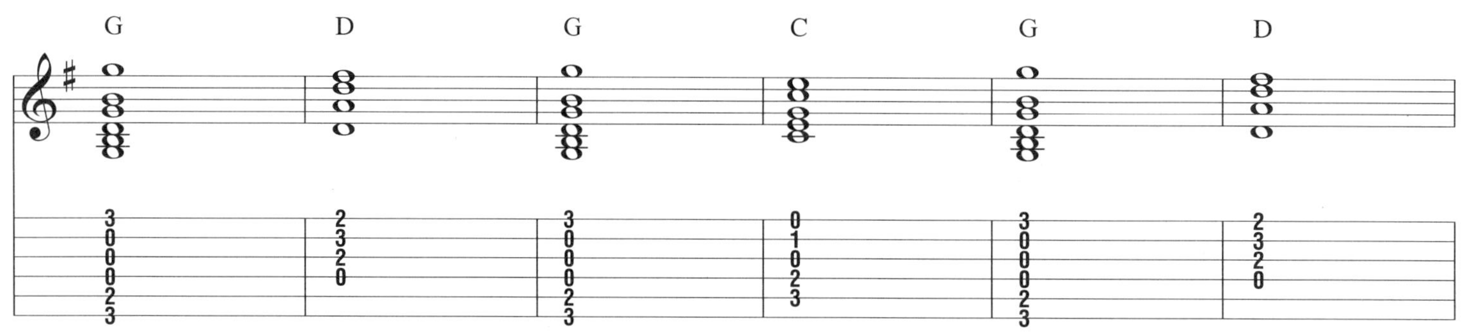

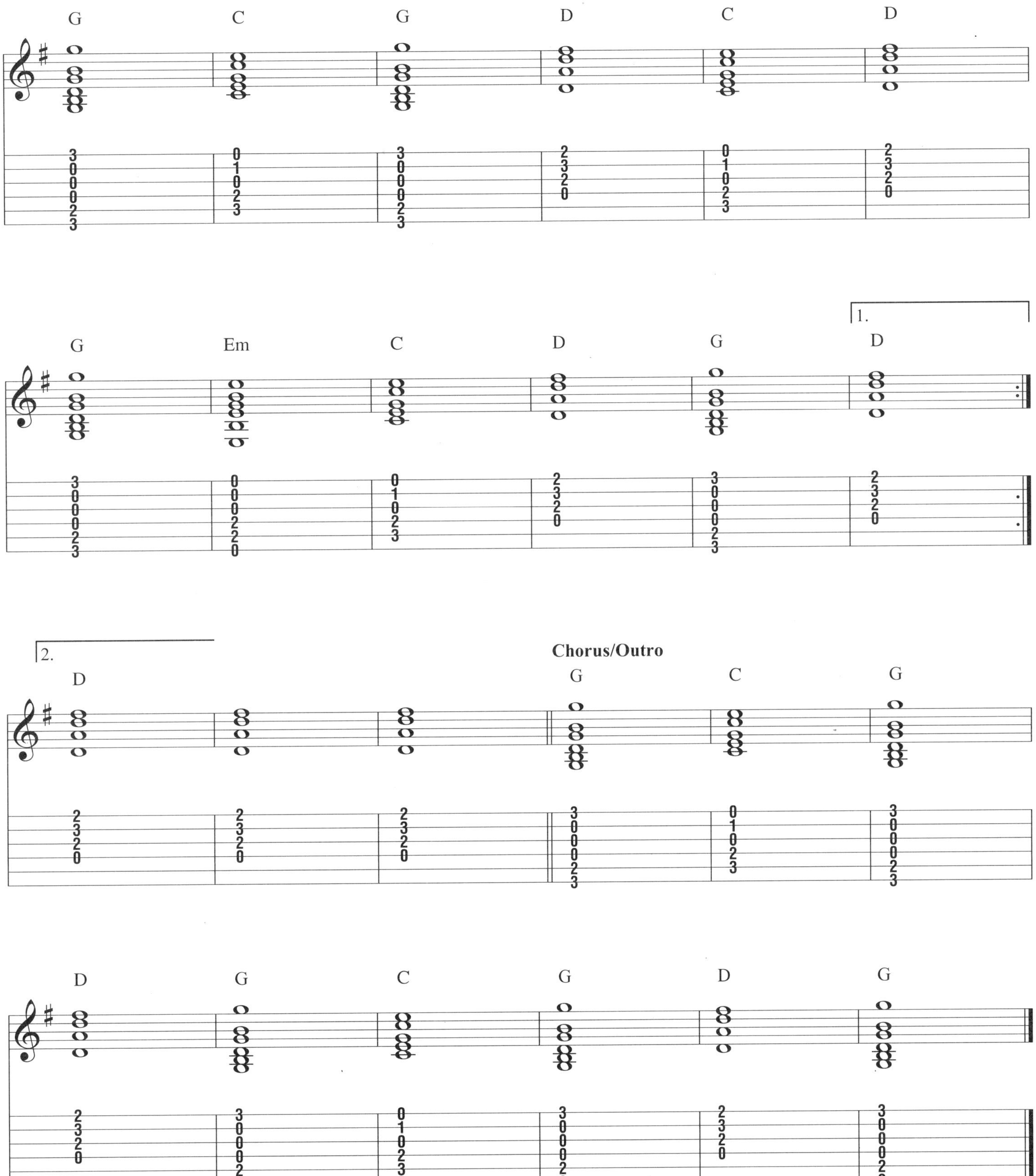
G C G D C D
G Em C D G D
1.
2.
D
Chorus/Outro
G C G
D G C G D G

For the next song, we're going to learn some variations of the G and C chords, namely, a four-fingered G chord and a Cadd9 chord. These chords are super popular in a variety of musical styles because not only do they sound great, but the transition between them is super easy.

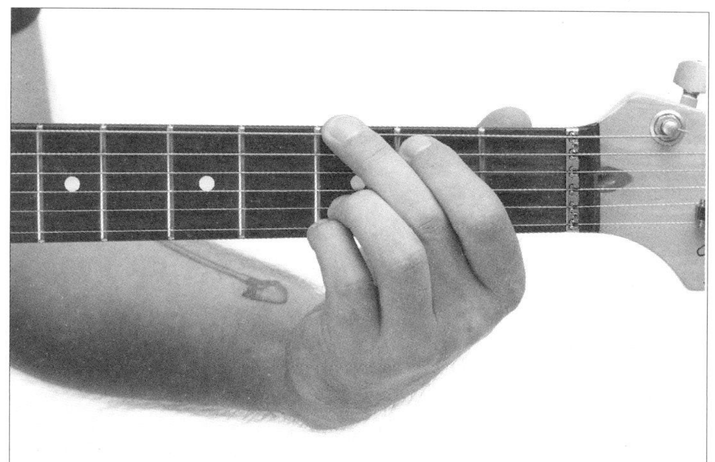

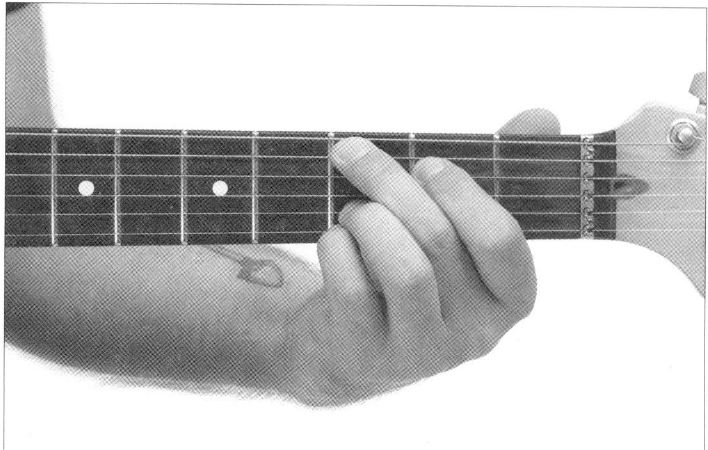

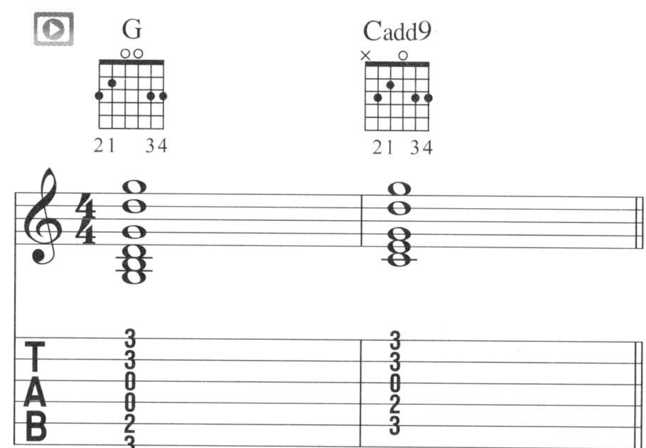

As you can see, the third and fourth fingers are common to both chords, so we can leave those fingers down when switching between the chords. All we need to do is keep the first and second fingers in the same shape and move them from one set of strings to the next.

You might be wondering, "How do we know which version of G to play if the chord name for both versions is G?" Well, in most cases, songs will list the chord shapes they want you to use at the beginning. But if you just get letter names, it's up to you to decide. Both versions musically act as a G chord and are interchangeable from a theory standpoint. In general, we'll decide which one to use based on the sound we want or the chord we're transitioning to or from. Now, the Cadd9 chord is a different story. That one is not interchangeable with a C chord. It has a similar sound, but from a theory standpoint it contains different notes than the C chord.

Let's put these new chords together in the popular acoustic tune from Green Day, "Good Riddance (Time of Your Life)." Right now, we'll just strum one chord for each measure. (In a few chapters, however, we'll learn the actual strum pattern for the song and make it sound just like the original recording!) Again, try to anticipate the chord changes so that you can make them happen in time with the music. Use the *tempo* (speed) on the audio as a goal to get those chord changes made in time. The chord frames are shown above the song for reference.

RHYTHM NOTATION

When strumming chords, we'll use a new system of notation called rhythm notation. To keep things simple and focused on the rhythm, we'll show the chord name and then use diamond- and slash-shaped note heads for the strums.

GOOD RIDDANCE

(Time of Your Life)

Words by Billie Joe
Music by Green Day

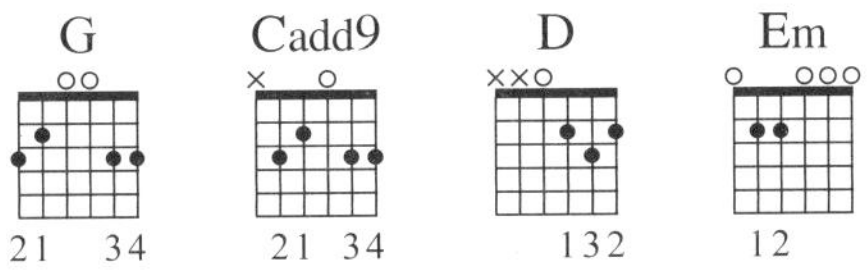

G Cadd9 D Em C

21 34 | 21 34 | 132 | 12 | 32 1

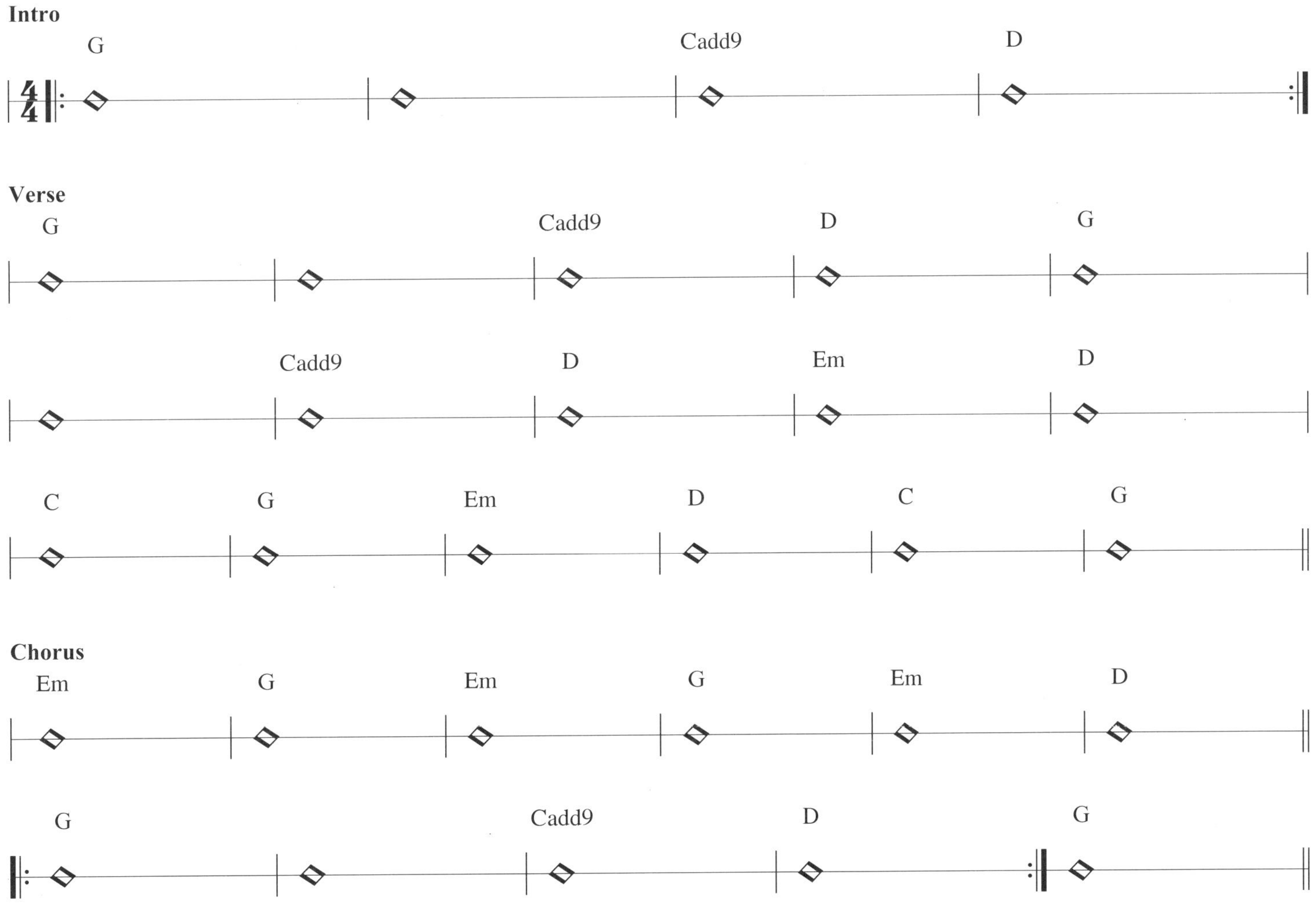

Intro

4/4 G | | Cadd9 | D :|

Verse

G | | Cadd9 | D | G |

| Cadd9 | D | Em | D |

C | G | Em | D | C | G ||

Chorus

Em | G | Em | G | Em | D ||

G | | Cadd9 | D :| G ||

Let's add another new chord to our repertoire, the Am chord. This chord shares two fingers with the C chord shape. In fact, try forming the C chord and then move the third finger to fret 2 on the third string (A). This is the Am chord.

Now try playing the Am chord in the popular Vance Joy hit, "Riptide." Again, we'll keep the strums simple for now since learning to change chords does take some time.

Words and Music by Vance Joy

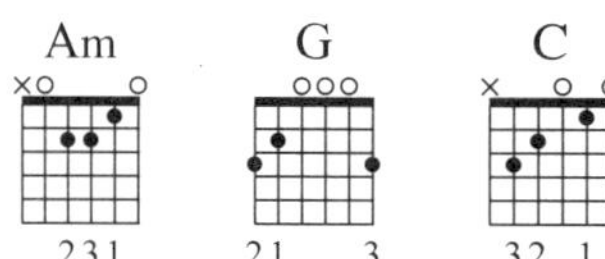

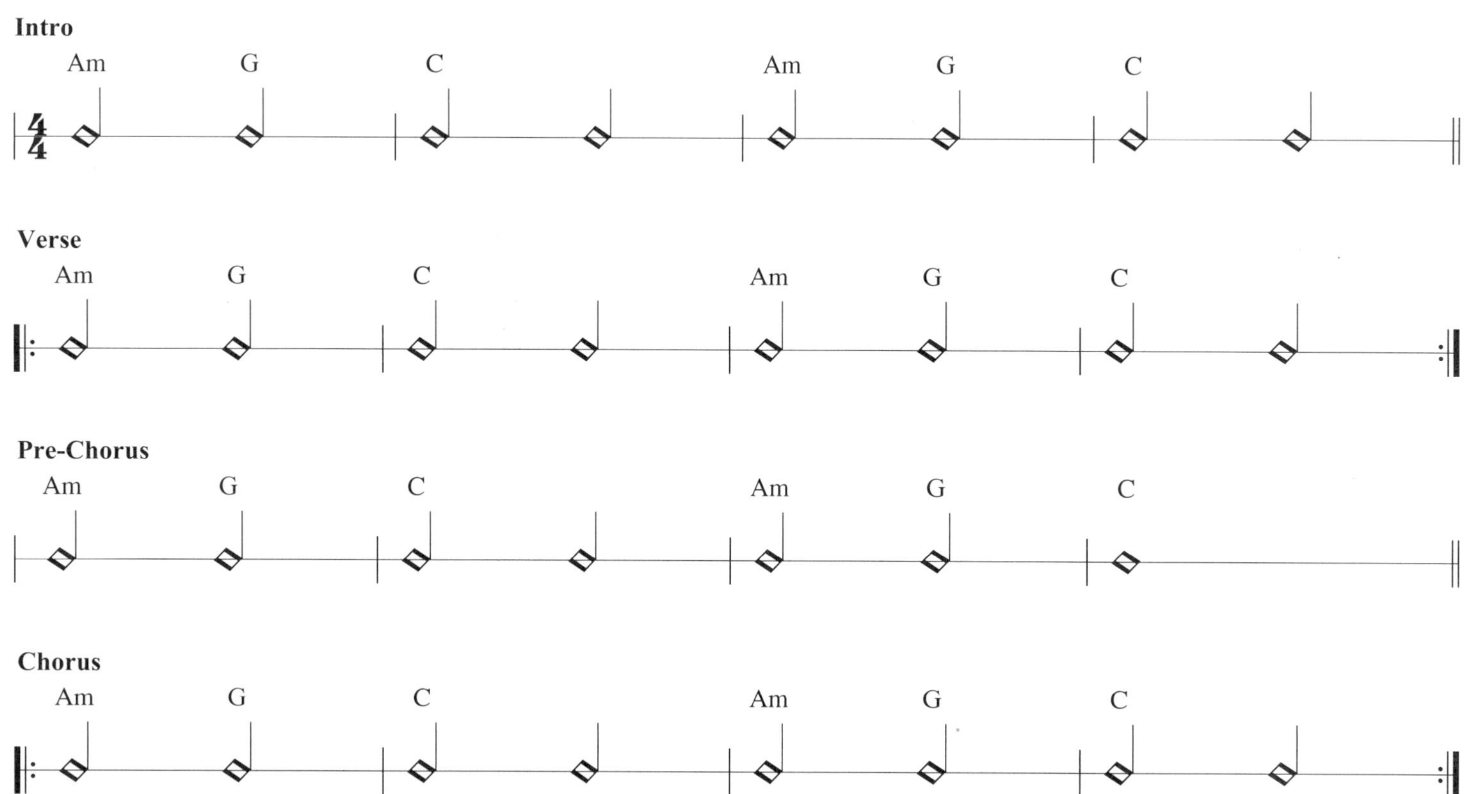

We'll finish off this chapter with the Ed Sheeran favorite, "Perfect." This song is in a new time signature, 12/8, which tells us that there are twelve beats per measure (12) and the eighth note (8), not the quarter note, receives one beat. Sounds tricky, right? Well, it's easier to play in 12/8 than it sounds. While the eighth note does receive one beat in 12/8, we actually alter how we count and feel each measure. If we were to count every beat, it would be "1-2-3-4-5-6-7-8-9-10-11-12." But that's a little cluttered and hard to follow. Instead, we still feel and count four beats in 12/8 by grouping three eighth notes together within each beat. So, we count "1-2-3-4," slowly, but each count is subdivided into three beats: **1**-2-3, **2**-2-3, **3**-2-3, **4**-2-3. Just to get a feel for playing in the new time signature, let's try a bit of the melody from "Perfect" first.

Words and Music by Ed Sheeran

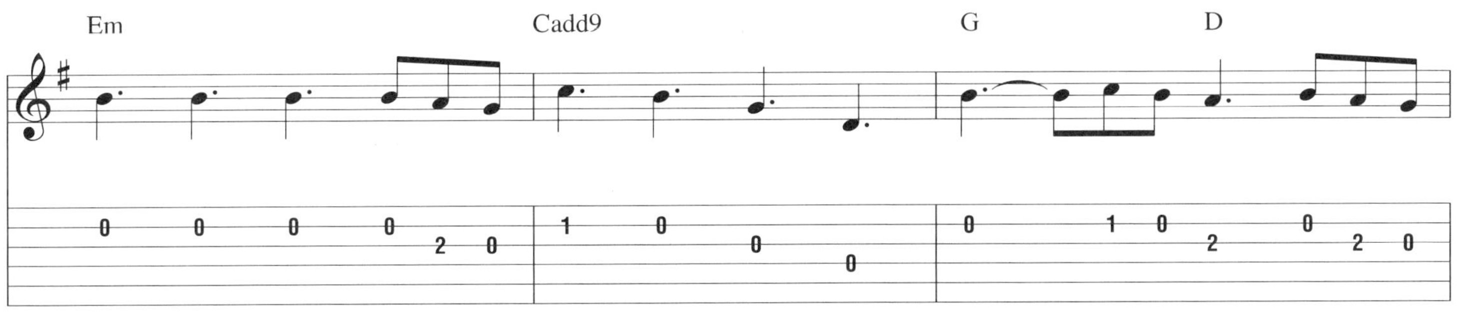

When we count "1-2-3-4" in 12/8, we're actually counting dotted quarter notes, since three eighth notes are included in the subdivision of each number. So, in the next arrangement of "Perfect," the rhythm you see for the strumming (all dotted quarter notes) is just telling you to strum a chord on each "1-2-3-4" beat. A dotted half note fills half a measure, and a dotted whole note fills a whole measure. The count-in on the included audio will give you the "1-2-3-4" (or the dotted quarter notes). This one will be more of a challenge than the last few songs we played chords on since we're strumming more frequently, leaving us with less time between the chord changes.

PERFECT

(Chords)

Words and Music by Ed Sheeran

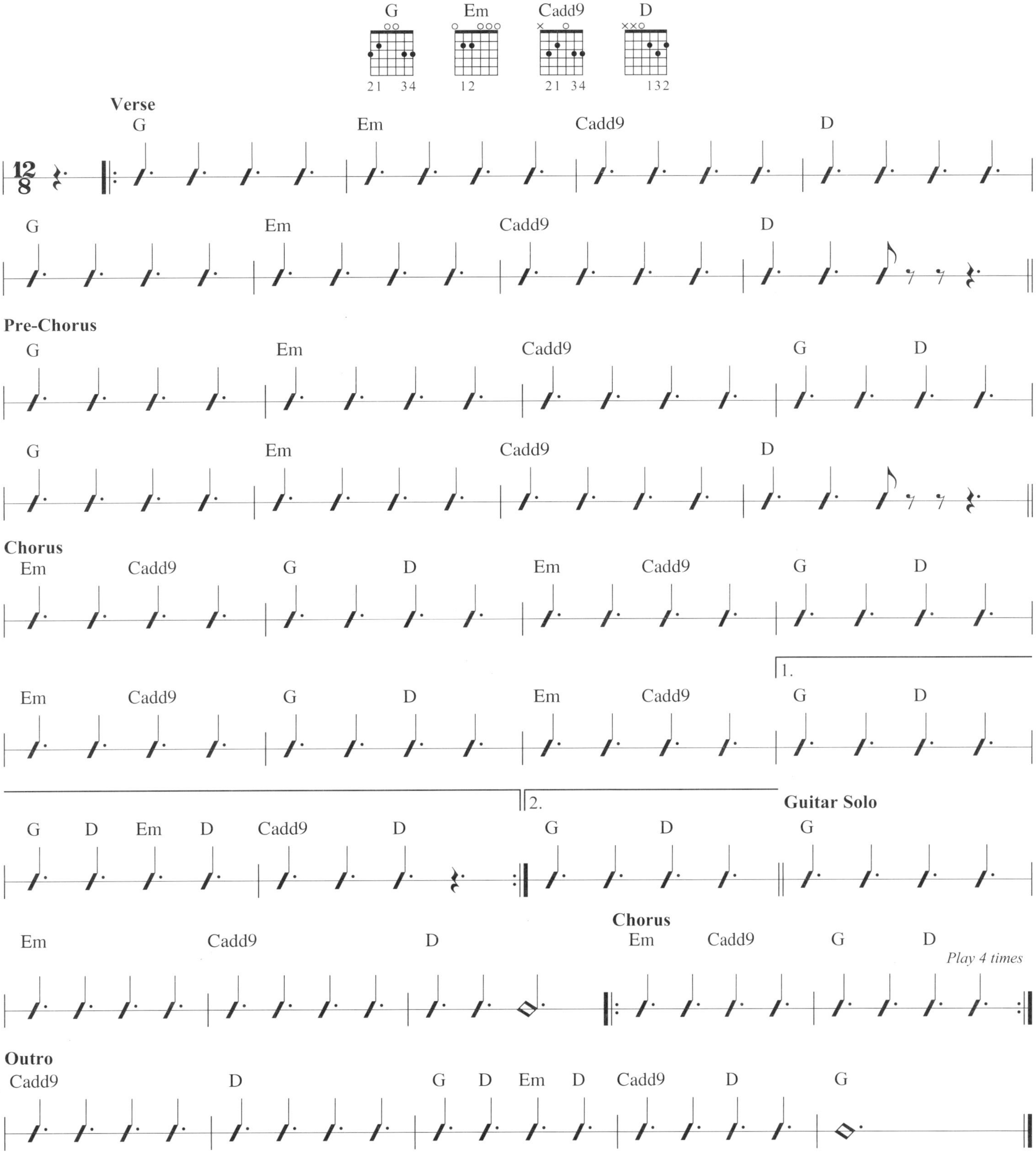

G Em Cadd9 D

21 34 · 12 · 21 34 · 132

Verse

G Em Cadd9 D

G Em Cadd9 D

Pre-Chorus

G Em Cadd9 G D

G Em Cadd9 D

Chorus

Em Cadd9 G D Em Cadd9 G D

Em Cadd9 G D Em Cadd9 1. G D

G D Em D Cadd9 D 2. G D

Guitar Solo

G

Em Cadd9 D

Chorus

Em Cadd9 G D

Play 4 times

Outro

Cadd9 D G D Em D Cadd9 D G

CHAPTER 5: ARPEGGIOS

When we discussed playing each note of a chord individually to make sure all the notes were ringing out clearly, we were actually talking about playing an arpeggio. Simply put, an *arpeggio* is a "broken chord" where the notes are played individually, rather than all at once like when we strum. Although arpeggios can be used in soloing, we'll be exploring how to use them with chords as an accompaniment. Let's take a look at a simple arpeggio using a C chord. Note the suggested picking pattern and hold down the C chord the entire time.

EXERCISE 30

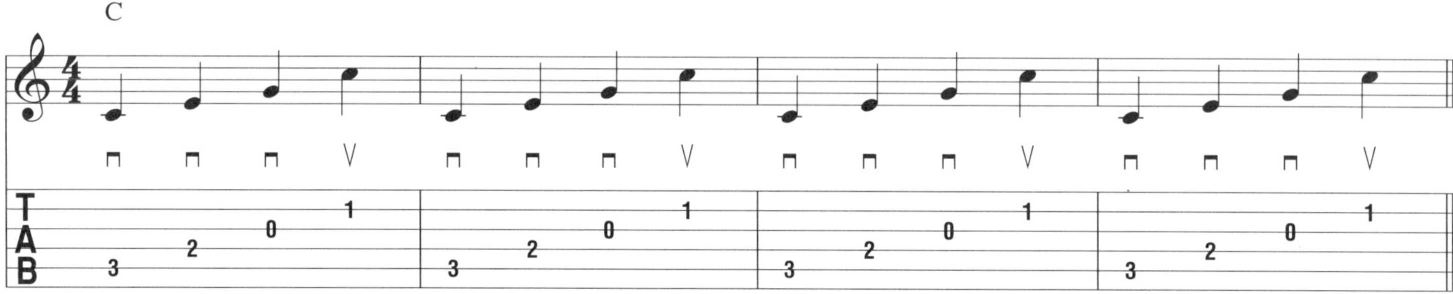

That was an ascending arpeggio, as the notes went from low to high. Although you can really use any picking pattern you'd like (all downstrokes, alternating, etc.), the suggested picking pattern we just used is very efficient. Playing the highest note with an upstroke allows the pick to travel naturally back to the low note using less motion in the picking hand.

We can also play an arpeggio in a descending style, from high to low. This time we'll start with upstrokes, and the downstroke on the lowest note will help get us back to the start of the pattern.

EXERCISE 31

Arpeggios don't have to follow any specific structure. They're really just the notes of a chord played separately. Rhythms can vary and the patterns can be more random.

EXERCISE 32

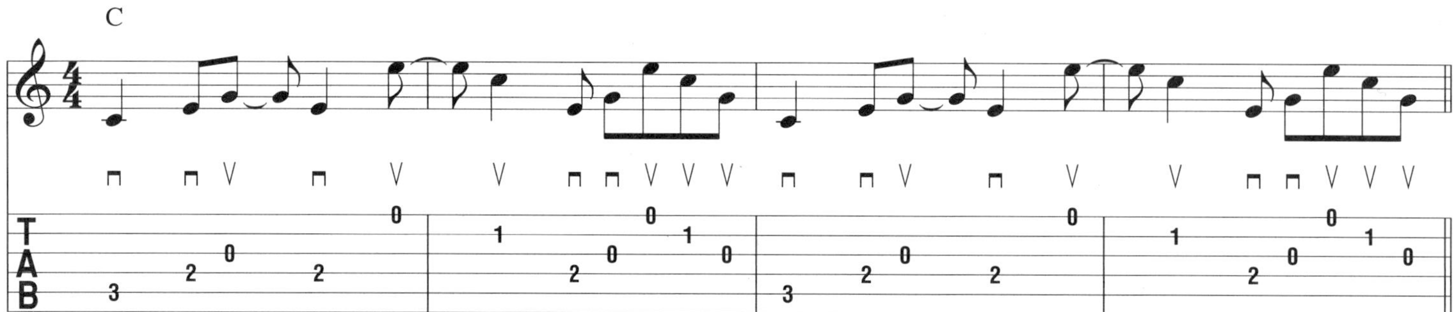

Again, the suggested picking pattern we just used keeps the right hand moving efficiently. But there is no right or wrong way to do it, so feel free to explore other options. Just realize that even though a suggested technique may feel awkward at first, in time it will become second nature. So, be careful not to just settle on what feels easiest right away. Sometimes those easy techniques will limit what we can do as the music gets more difficult.

Let's try a few arpeggios along with some chord changes. Notice that we'll skip the fifth string when we play a chord with its root note on the sixth string. Be sure to hold down each chord for the entire measure.

EXERCISE 33

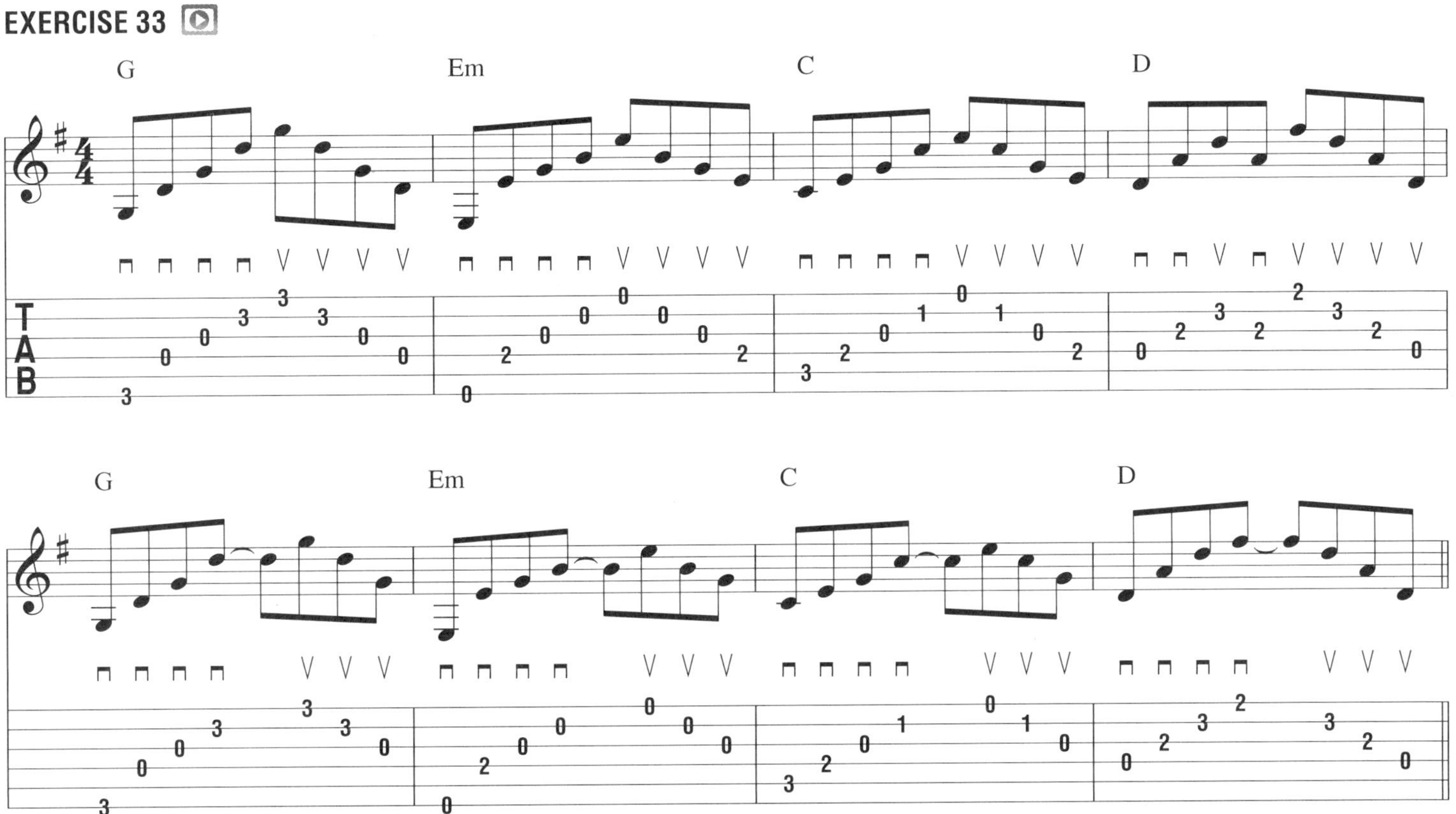

In addition to playing the notes of a chord as an arpeggio, we can also add additional notes not found in the original chord. To do this, we keep holding down the chord and choose an unused finger for the extra note.

EXERCISE 34

You can even play arpeggio riffs for chord shapes you're not familiar with. In the next exercise, just pay attention to the tab and hold down all the notes in every measure before beginning each one.

EXERCISE 35

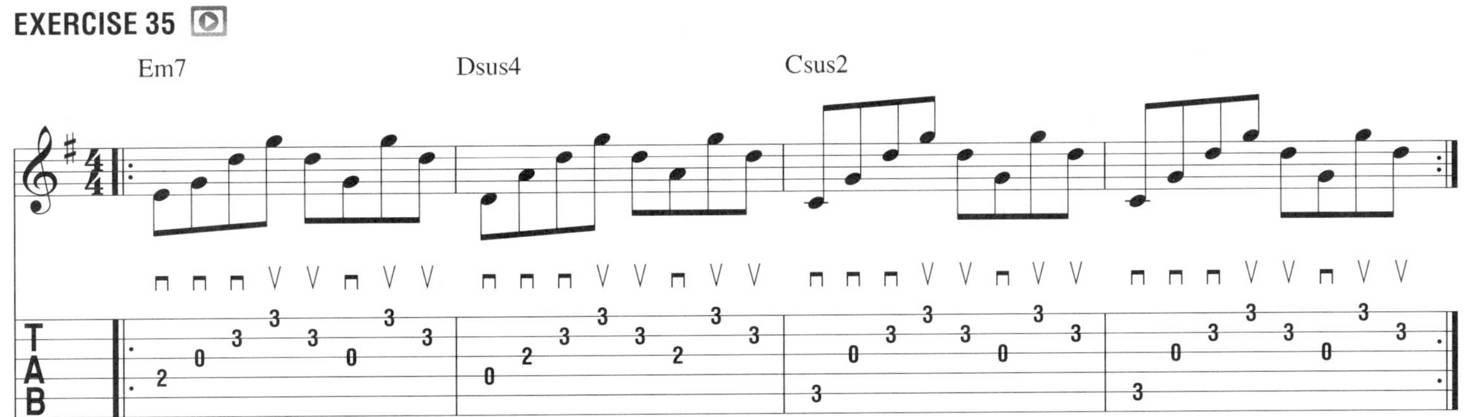

Before we play our final song of the chapter, we need to learn one more new chord, B7. We won't need to hold down all the notes of the B7 chord to play the upcoming song, but it's a great habit to get into anyway. That's because even if an arpeggio doesn't use every note of a chord, holding down the full chord is a nice safety net in case you accidentally hit the wrong string—at least the note you didn't mean to play will be part of the chord and should still sound good.

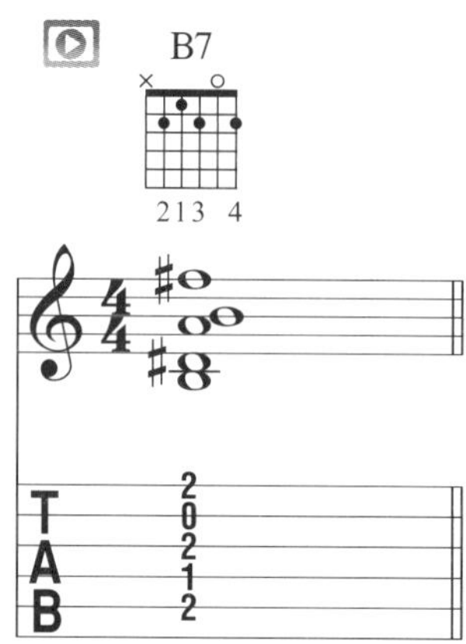

Now let's put our new arpeggio skills to use in the Leonard Cohen classic, "Hallelujah." The arpeggiated intro, famously used by Jeff Buckley in his cover of the song, is instantly recognizable. As soon as you hear it, you know exactly what song it is. To give you a little more practice figuring out the best chord shapes to hold down in a measure, as we did in exercise 35, the chord frames are not included above this song. This song uses a 6/8 time signature, meaning there are six beats per measure (6) and the eighth note (8) gets the beat. We count it kind of like 12/8, but this time we only count "1-2" (or **1**-2-3, **2**-2-3) for each measure. Notice that the first ending in this song is actually a "first-through-fourth" ending, so be sure to play all of the material within the repeat signs four times before skipping that ending and moving on to the next one. We also have a wavy arrow next to the last chord. This *arpeggiato* symbol simply tells us to strum the chord slowly in the direction of the arrow, kind of like a quick arpeggio.

CAPOS

If you want to play along with the original recording of "Hallelujah," you'll need a device called a capo. A *capo* is a mechanical clamp that holds down all six strings at the selected fret. In this case, the capo would be secured across fret 5 (but you won't need a capo to play along with our provided audio).

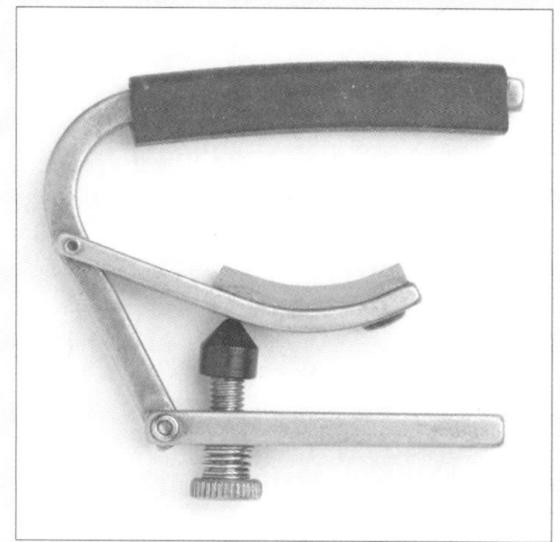

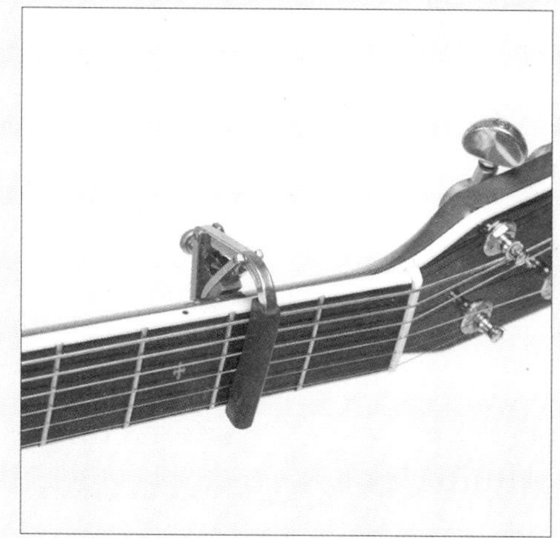

HALLELUJAH

Words and Music by Leonard Cohen

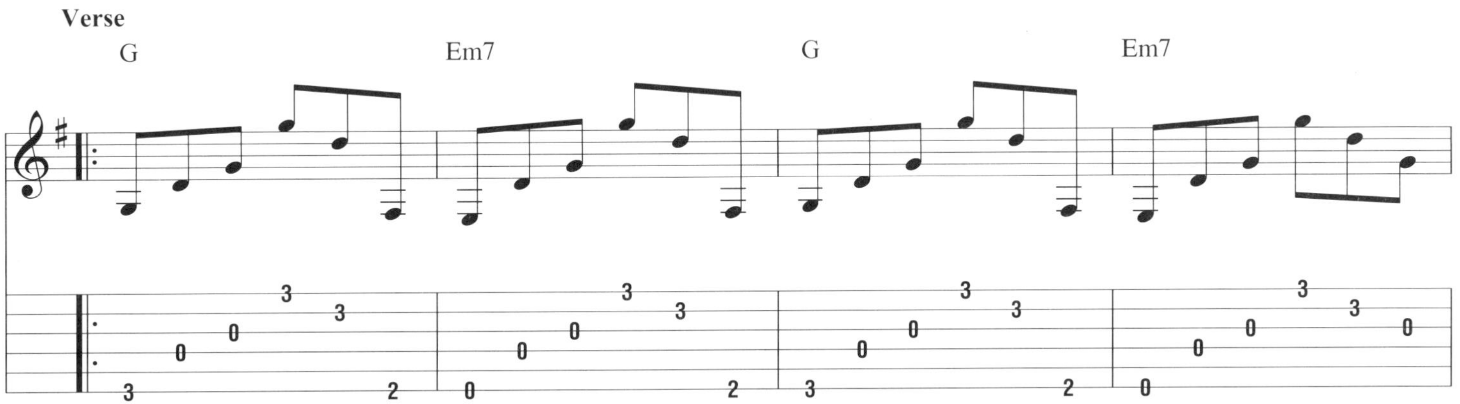

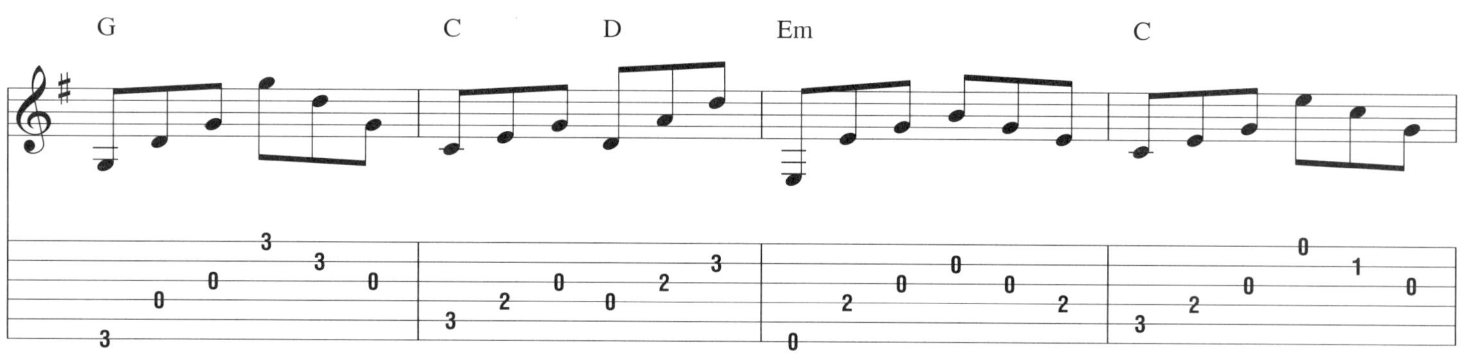

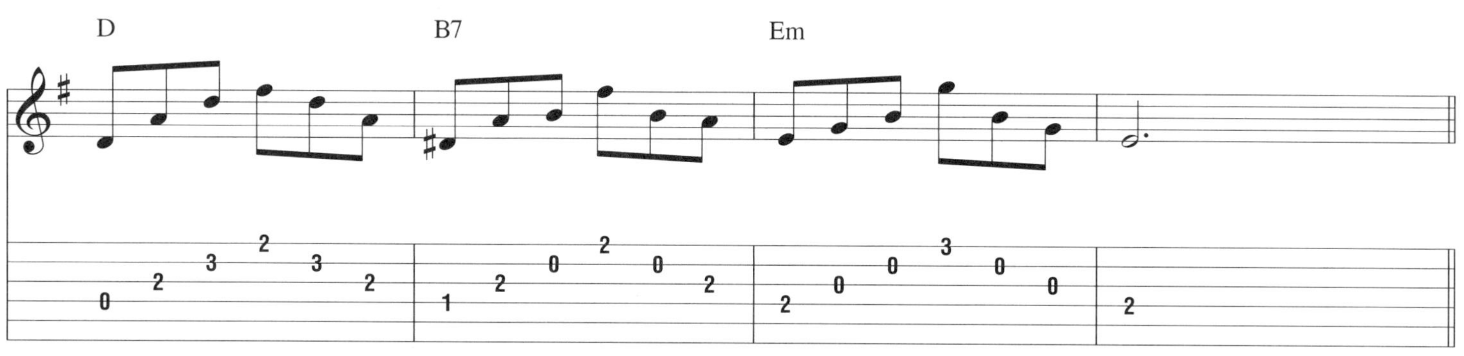

Chorus

1.–4.
Interlude
G
Em7
G
Em7
5.
Chorus
C
Em
C
G
D
Outro
G
Em7
G
Em7
G

CHAPTER 6: STRUM PATTERNS

Instead of just strumming with simple downstrokes, we can use the same alternate-picking concept we used for single notes and apply it to chords. By now, your chords should be feeling more comfortable, and switching between them should feel a bit easier, so let's start by looking at a simple eighth-note strum pattern on an Em chord.

EXERCISE 36

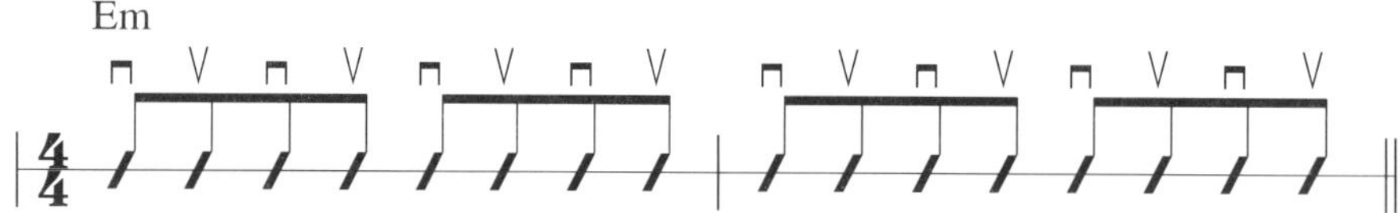

Now let's mix up the rhythm a bit using quarter notes and eighth notes.

EXERCISE 37

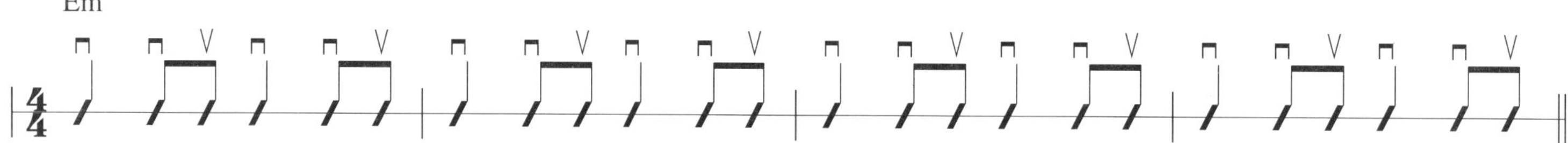

Here, we'll add some chord changes that move between Em and the three-finger G chord. Since we're also playing eighth notes in this rhythm (meaning the transitions will be more difficult than when we just played quarter notes), try to anticipate the chord changes and see the new chord shape you need to move to in advance.

EXERCISE 38

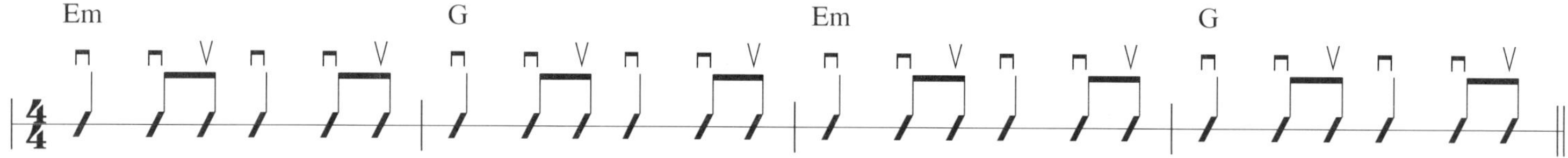

Next, we'll add a bit of syncopation to the strum pattern. *Syncopation* is when the music surprises you by stressing beats in places you don't expect (like on the upbeats, for example). The following syncopated strum pattern is a common one, used in many songs, in which you'll play two upstrokes in a row. In between those two upstrokes, the right hand should do a "missed" downstroke, in time, after the first one in order to get in position for the second one. So, the hand moves down as if playing a downstroke, but the pick doesn't contact any strings. Check out the video to see what this looks like.

EXERCISE 39

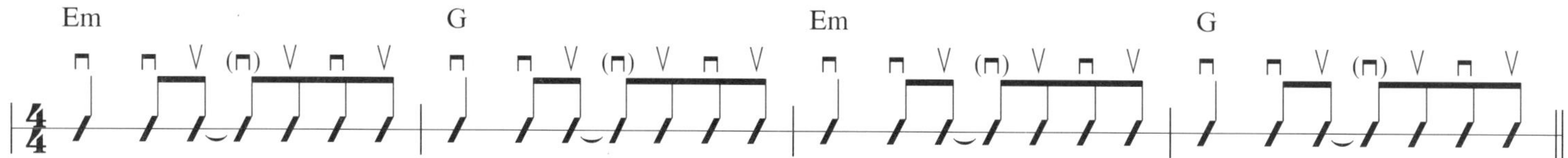

Now let's use this strum pattern in some songs. We'll revisit a few of the tunes we played back when we first learned chords and just used a simple downstroke rhythm, this time spicing it up with the real thing. First up is "Brown Eyed Girl." Now might be a good time to mention something we do sometimes to make chord changes easier. As you might be able to hear on the audio, we can often get away with strumming the strings open for the last chord in a measure. As long as the tempo is fast enough, and provided it doesn't sound bad, this is a common trick we use to get a little more time to reposition our left hand.

BROWN EYED GIRL

Words and Music by Van Morrison

G
C
D
Em
21 3
32 1
132
12

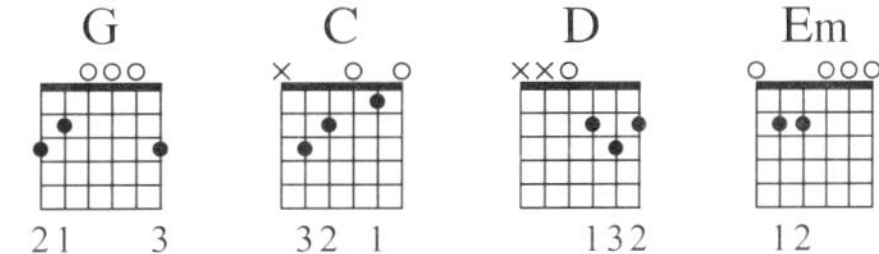

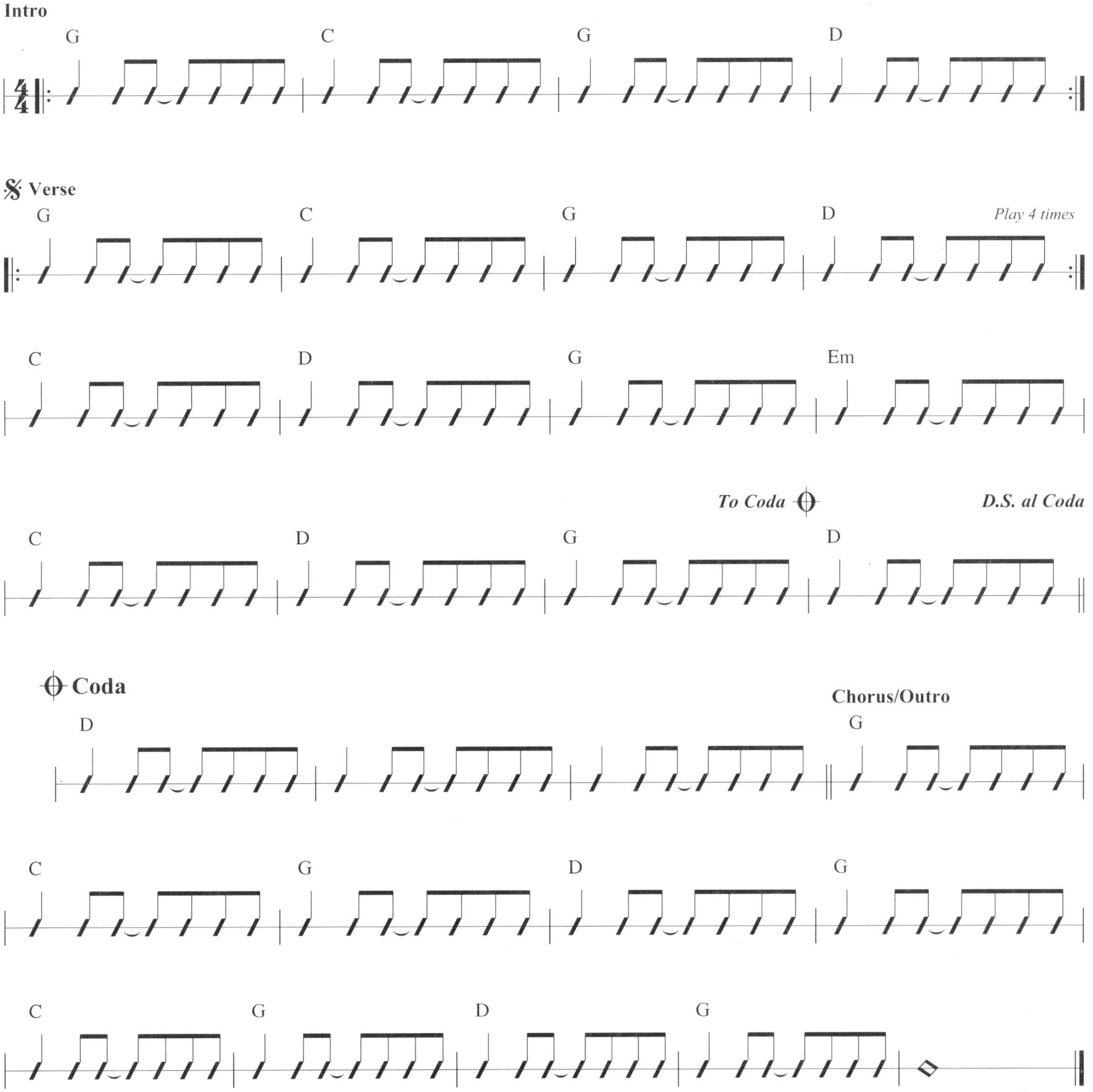

Intro
G
C
G
D
Verse
G
C
G
D
Play 4 times
C
D
G
Em
To Coda
D.S. al Coda
C
D
G
D
Coda
Chorus/Outro
D
G
C
G
D
G
C
G
D
G

That same strum pattern will work for "Good Riddance (Time of Your Life)." Be light and relaxed with your wrist and pick motions, and don't dig in too hard on the strings.

GOOD RIDDANCE
(Time of Your Life)

Words by Billie Joe
Music by Green Day

G
Cadd9
D
Em
C
21 34
21 34
132
12
32 1

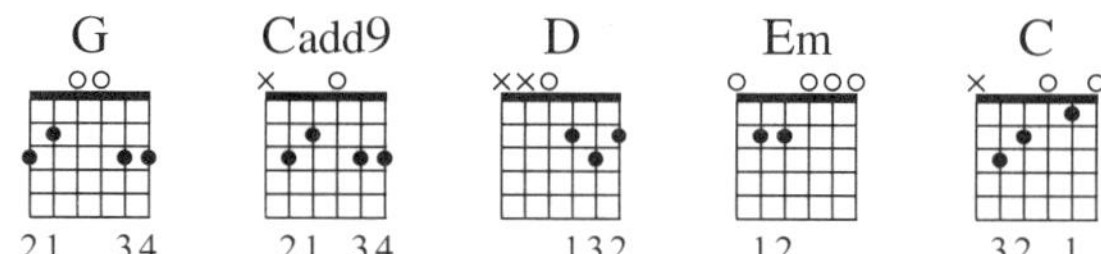

Intro

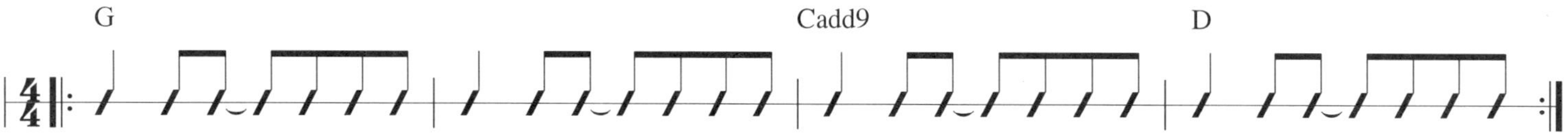

G
Cadd9
D

Verse

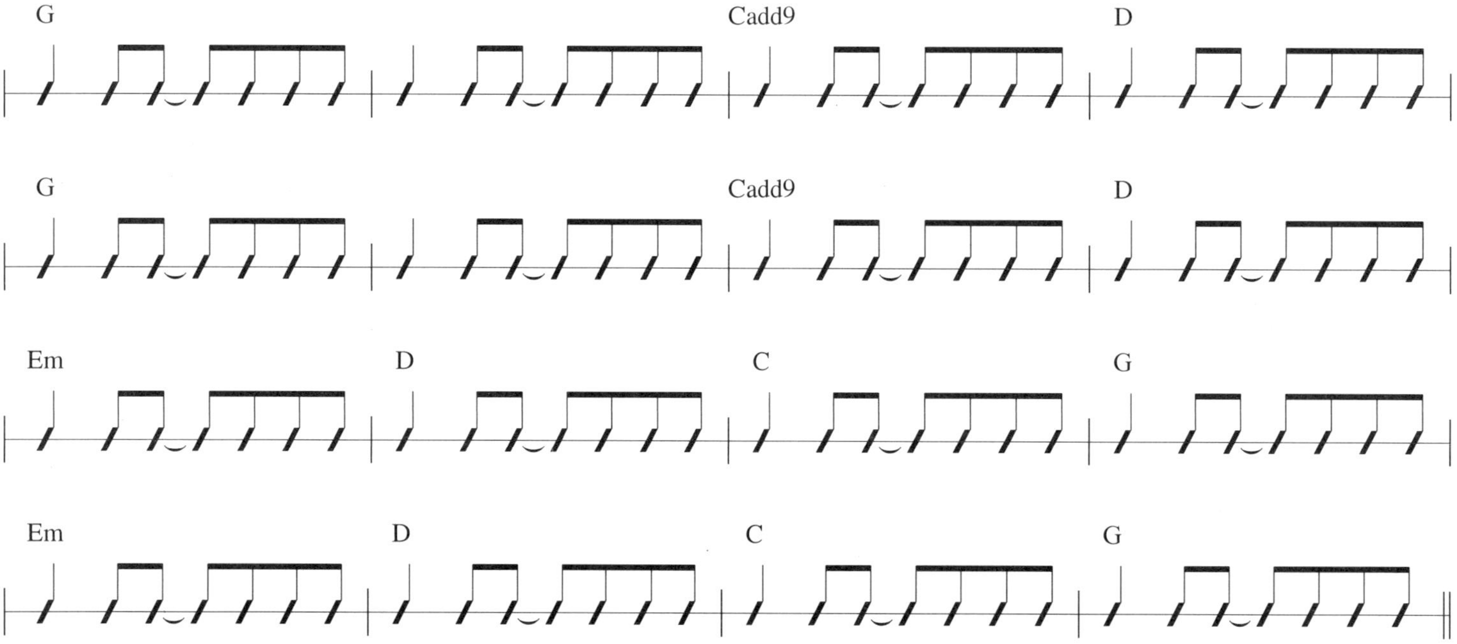

G
Cadd9
D
G
Cadd9
D
Em
D
C
G
Em
D
C
G

Chorus

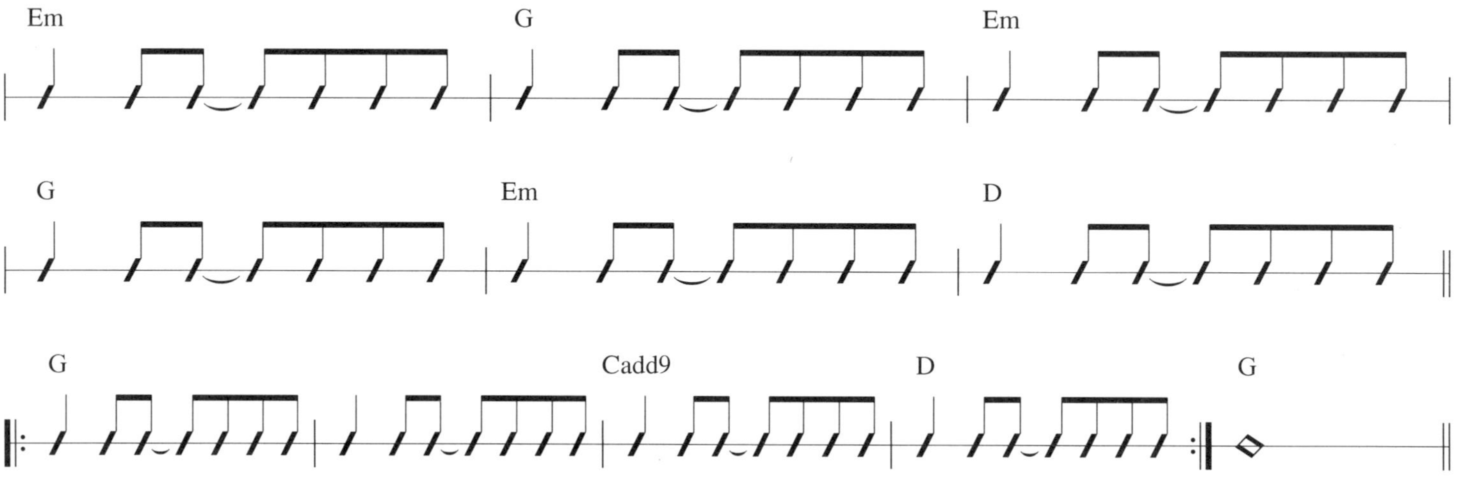

Em
G
Em
G
Em
D
G
Cadd9
D
G

SIXTEENTH NOTES

Just like the way two eighth notes make up one quarter note, we can get two *sixteenth notes* by dividing the eighth note in half. And similar to the way eighth notes look, sixteenth notes can be either written with two flags 𝅘𝅥𝅯 or connected with a double beam ♬♬. To count sixteenth notes, we add the syllables "e" (pronounced "ee") and "a" (pronounced "uh") to the count, giving us "1-e-&-a-2-e-&-a-3-e-&-a-4-e-&-a." Sixteenth notes go by even faster than eighth notes, so again alternate picking is the right choice. Let's try a simple exercise using quarter, eighth, and sixteenth notes.

EXERCISE 40

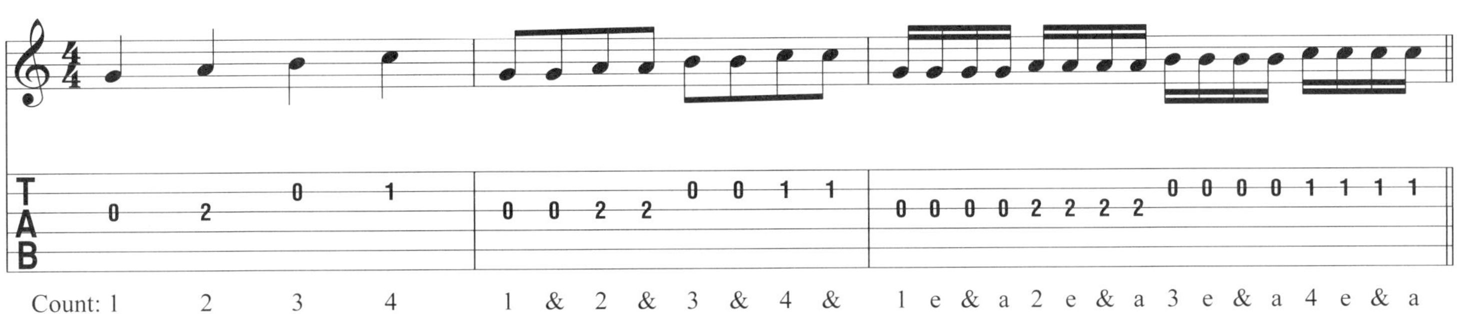

Let's try out an arpeggio pattern with sixteenth notes. Remember, since a dot adds one half the value of the note, the *dotted eighth notes* you see in the exercise will be worth three sixteenth notes.

EXERCISE 41

G Em C D

G Em C D

G Em C D

Let's go back and play "Riptide" using some sixteenth notes in the strum pattern. Now that we've divided the beat down to sixteenth notes, which we'll play with a down-up pattern, the eighth notes will be your downstrokes. When strumming, we always want to preserve that perpetual motion of the hand keeping time with the beats.

RIPTIDE

Words and Music by Vance Joy

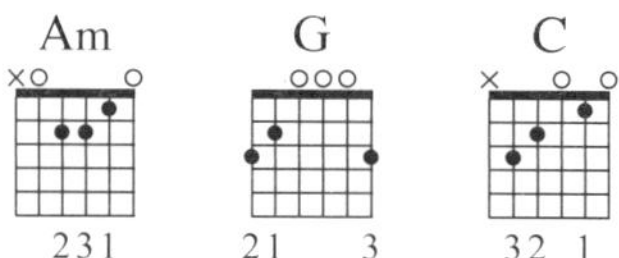

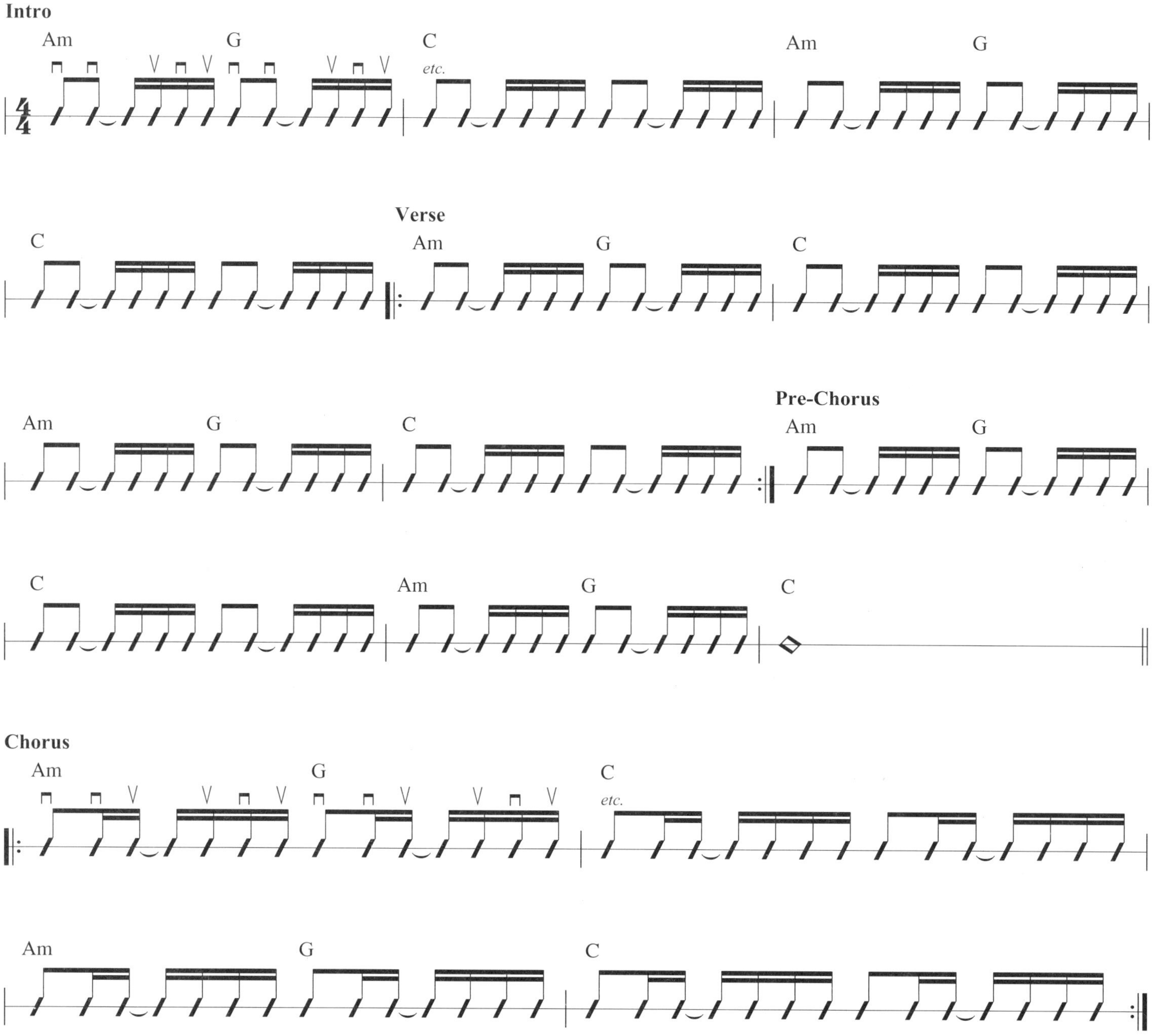

Intro

Am G C *etc.* Am G

C

Verse

Am G C

Am G C

Pre-Chorus

Am G

C Am G C

Chorus

Am G C *etc.*

Am G C

MUTED STRUMS

Have you ever heard those scratchy, percussive-like sounds in a guitar part and wondered what they were? We call them *muted strums*. To execute a muted strum, lay your left-hand fingers lightly across the strings, making sure not to press hard enough to fret them, and then strum normally with your right hand to get that "chick" sound. If you hear any open notes ringing, make sure your left hand is completely covering the strings. If you hear any fretted notes, just release the pressure a bit. In tab, a muted note will be notated with an "X." In rhythm notation and standard notation, an "X" note head will be used in place of a regular one.

Let's try this technique in the following rhythmic exercise. It's not too important where you place your fingers in regard to the frets, but for now, we'll stick to the first-four-frets area of the fretboard. Check out the video to see exactly how it's done.

EXERCISE 42

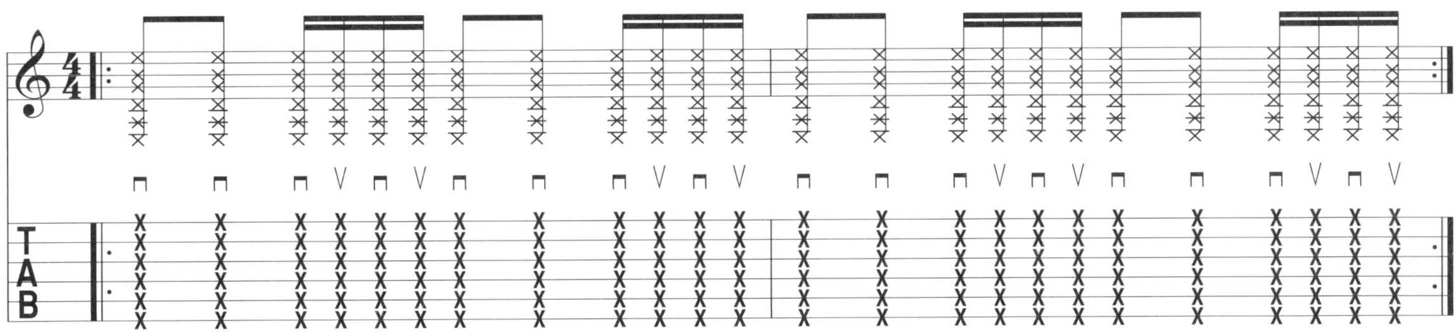

Oftentimes, muted strums are mixed in with fretted chords. In the next exercise, fret the chords and strum them as usual. For the muted strums, take your fingers off the chord you're playing and lay them across the strings. As you get more comfortable with this technique, you'll find that you'll be able to just flatten or collapse your fingers after fretting a chord to get a muted strum.

EXERCISE 43

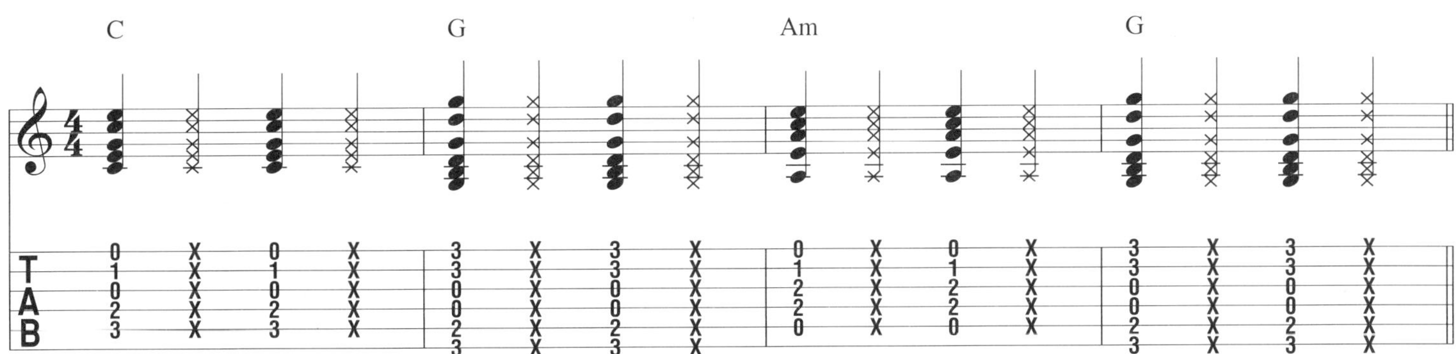

Now let's try some muted strums in the classic Nirvana tune, "Smells Like Teen Spirit." Since this one uses power chords and each chord includes two fretted notes, you can simply just release the pressure you're using on these chords a bit, keeping your fingers in the same position, to get the muted strum.

SMELLS LIKE TEEN SPIRIT

Words and Music by Kurt Cobain,
David Grohl, and Krist Novoselic

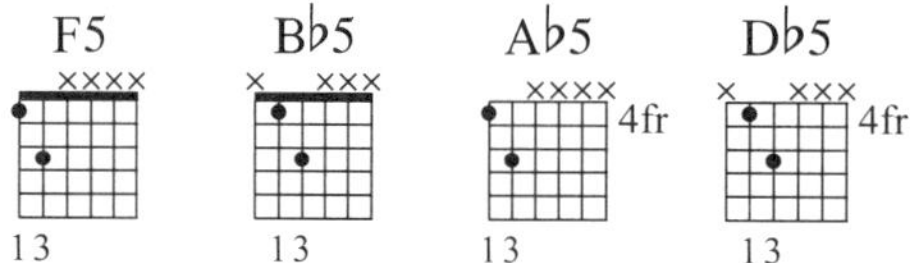

Before we conclude this chapter, let's learn a few new chords. For the F chord, we barre across the first fret on strings one and two with the first finger.

EXERCISE 44

Now for the final song of the chapter, the Beatles classic, "Hey Jude." You'll be reaching for some higher notes in the melody! First, though, work on the strum pattern and chords. Notice that the time signature changes to 2/4 for a measure. This means that you'll count "1-2," not "1-2-3-4," for that measure. We again have an F♯ in the key signature, meaning we play every F a fret higher unless we see a natural sign on one of them. Instead of writing out the strum pattern in the song itself, we'll just include it once here. You'll use this pattern exclusively.

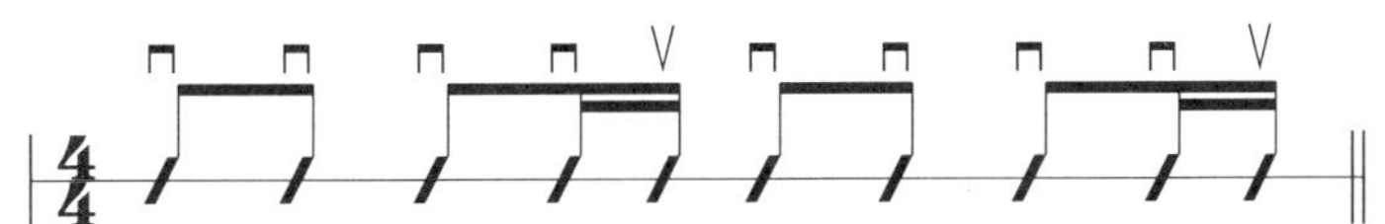

HEY JUDE

Words and Music by John Lennon
and Paul McCartney

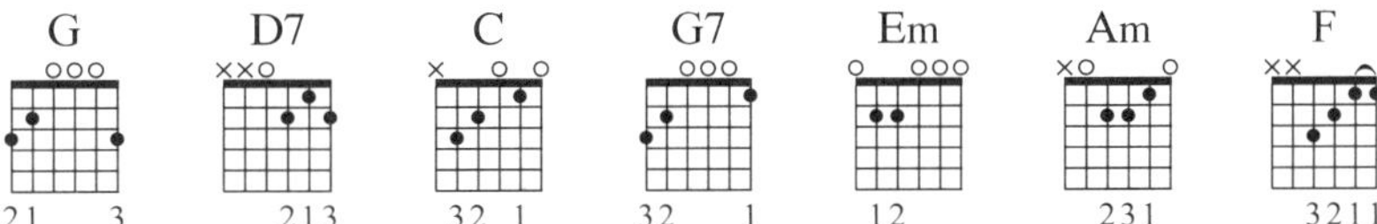

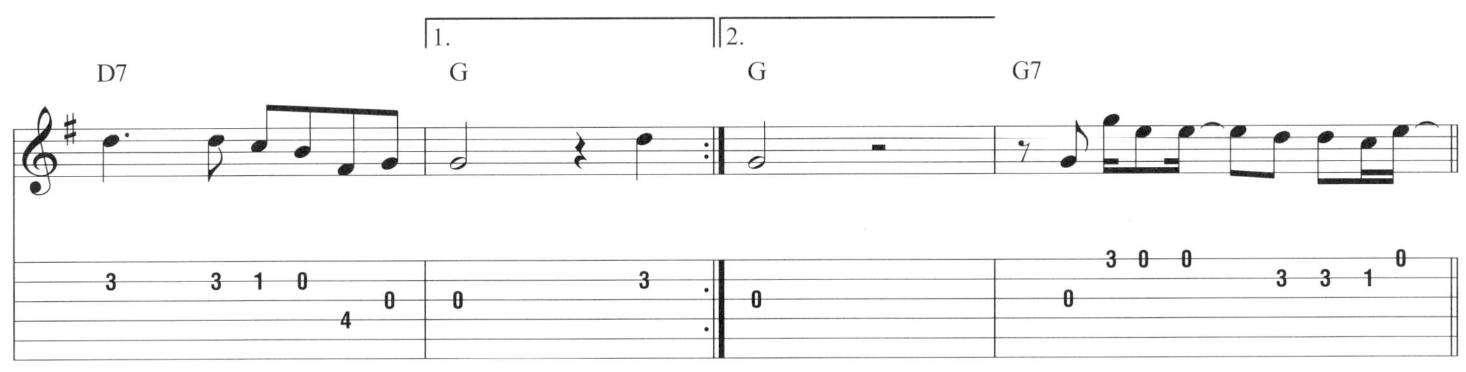

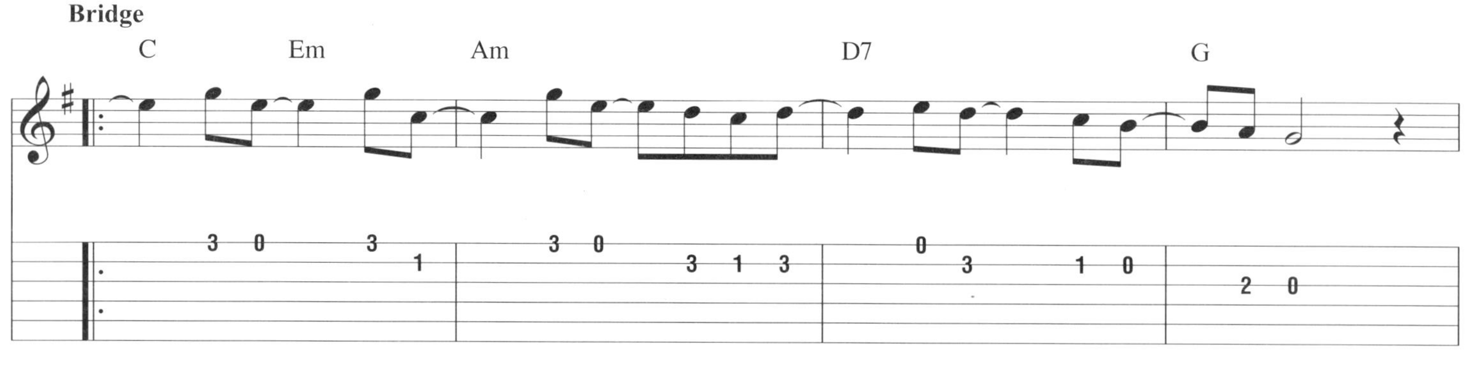
Bridge
C
Em
Am
D7
G

G7
C
Em
Am
D7

G
G7
D7

Verse
G
D7

G
C
G
1.
D7
G
G7

2.
D7
G

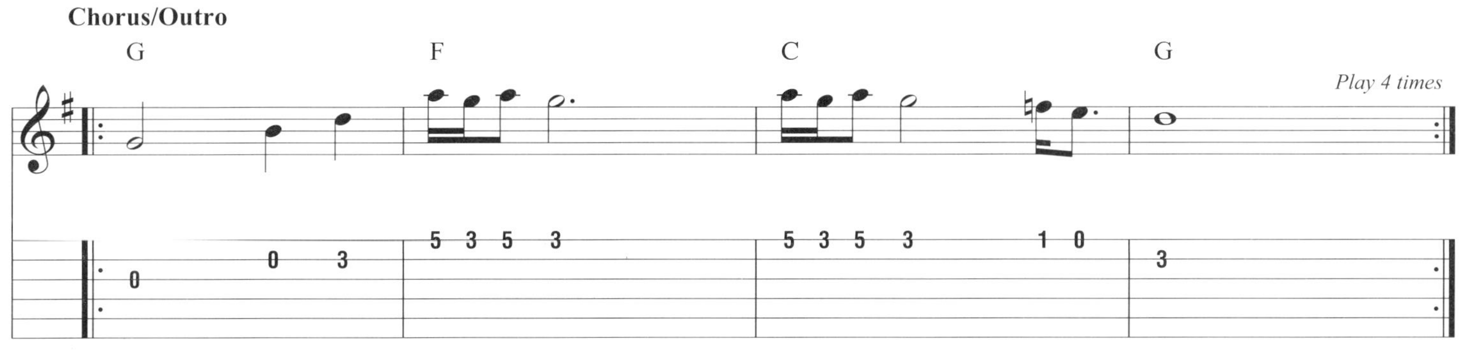
Chorus/Outro
G
F
C
G
Play 4 times

CHAPTER 7: FINGERSTYLE

Now it's time to put the pick away and learn a technique referred to as fingerstyle. When we play *fingerstyle*, we use the fingers of the right hand instead of a pick to pluck the strings. The thumb typically plays the three lowest strings. The index, middle, and ring fingers handle the third, second, and first strings, respectively. You'll find that you may need to deviate from this finger setup from time to time, but it's the general rule we follow.

In this chapter, we'll explore two common approaches to fingerstyle guitar: one that focuses on pure accompaniment patterns, similar to what you'd do when strumming, and another where you play both the melody and accompaniment together in a solo guitar arrangement. Additionally, we'll take a look at a style of fingerpicking known as "Travis picking."

FINGERSTYLE ACCOMPANIMENT

Let's try a very basic accompaniment pattern using a few chords we know. Notice that this is similar to playing arpeggios with a pick.

RIGHT-HAND FINGERING

In fingerstyle guitar, we use letters to identify the fingers of the right hand. These letters come from the Spanish names for the fingers and have been used for a very long time in classical guitar music.

p = thumb (*pulgar*) i = index (*índice*) m = middle (*medio*) a = ring (*anular*)

EXERCISE 45

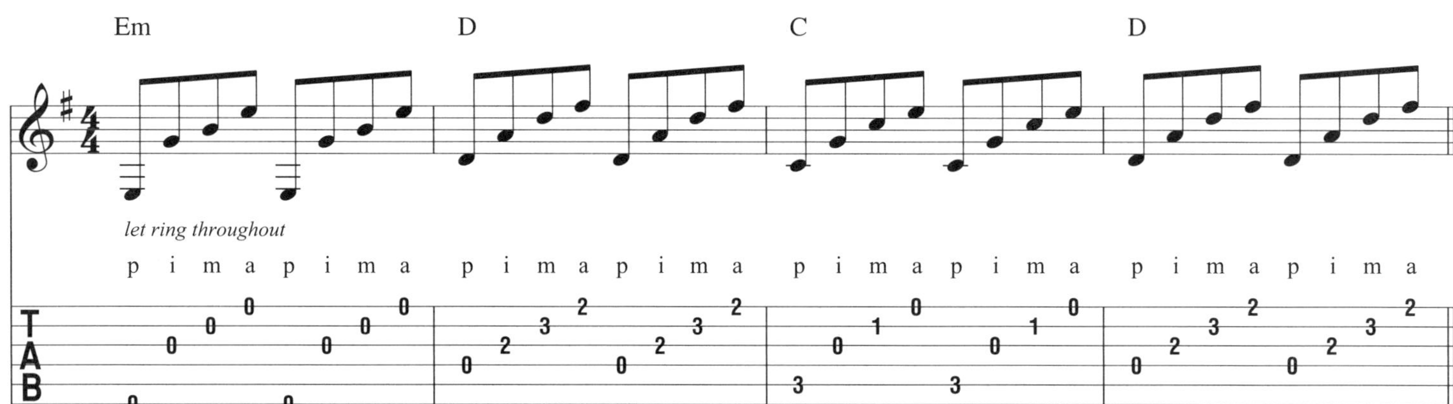

The next exercise mixes up the pattern a bit. Keep your right hand steady, try to avoid bouncing it up and down, and let the fingers do the work, mainly flexing from the big first-knuckle joint. When you take a look at the video for this exercise, focus your attention on the right hand to see this in action.

EXERCISE 46

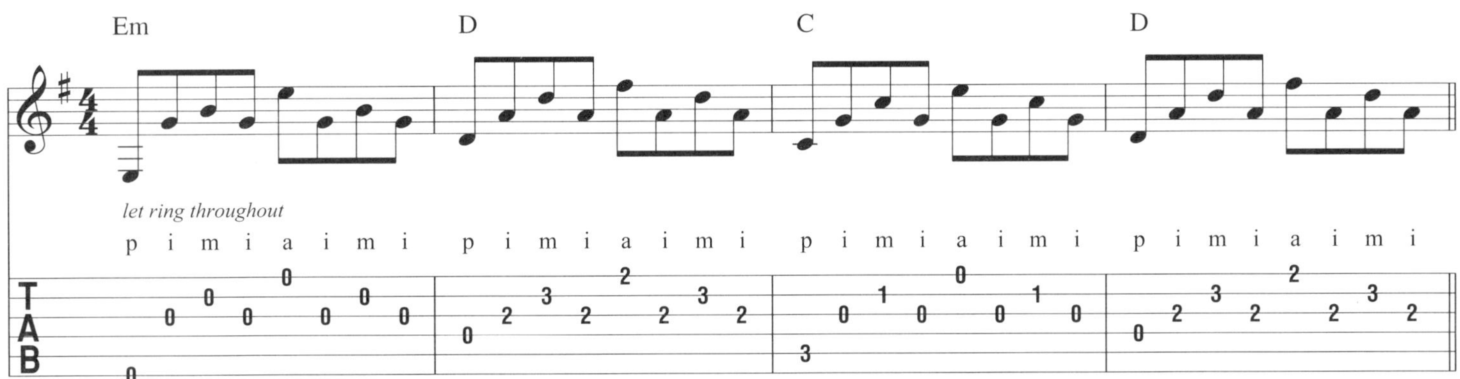

In addition to plucking single notes with the fingers, we can also fingerpick multiple notes at the same time. This gives us a different sound than the one we get when strumming, as all the notes are plucked simultaneously, unlike the slight delay between the notes that we hear when strumming. Let's try this out before diving into a tune. The goal in the next exercise is to pluck all of the strings in each of the chords at the same time, moving the fingers as one unit and aiming to keep them aligned and ready to land on the strings again.

EXERCISE 47

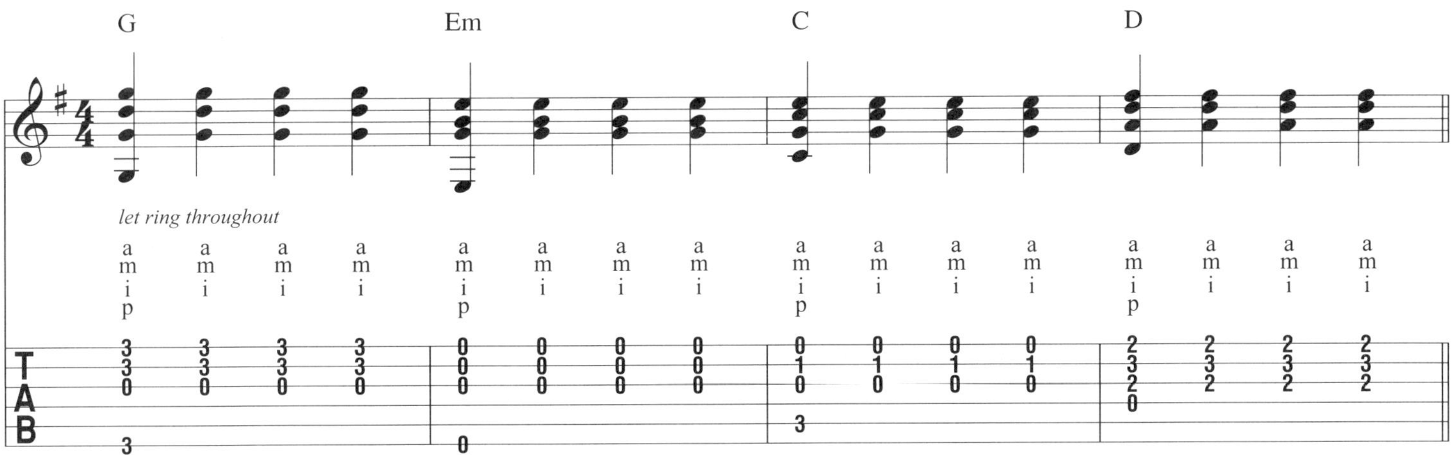

Now let's use this fingerpicking technique to revisit Ed Sheeran's "Perfect" and play the guitar part heard on the original recording. As before, we'll see right-hand fingering suggestions between the standard notation and tab. Note that the third finger of the left hand can stay planted on the D on the second string for the entire song—it's in every chord! Again, the click track on the included audio will give us "1-2-3-4," tracking the dotted quarter notes (or every three eighth notes). The symbol used over the last chord of the song is called a *fermata*, which simply tell us to hold that chord for longer than its written value.

PERFECT

Words and Music by Ed Sheeran

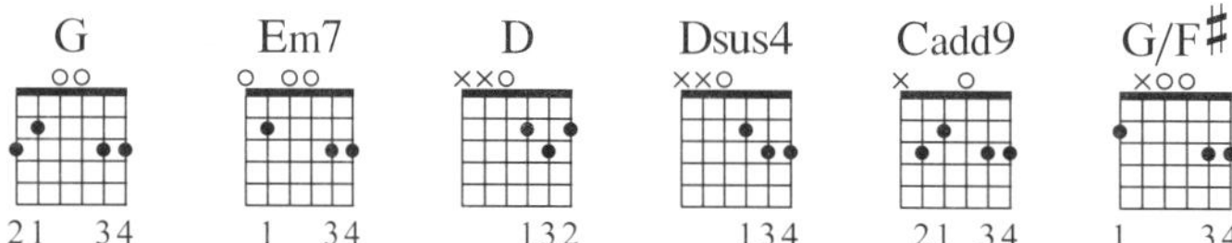

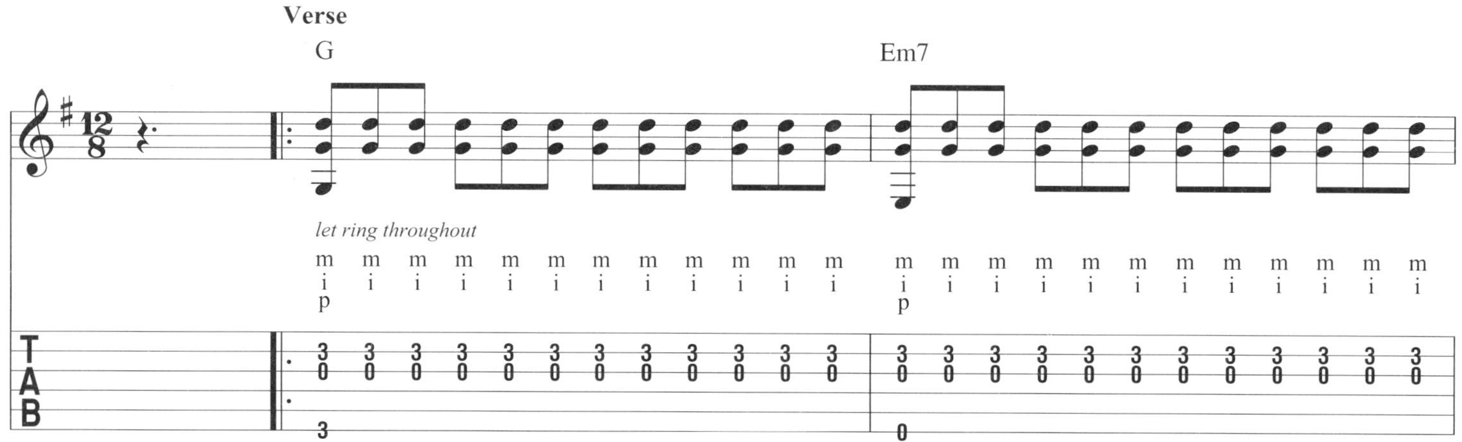

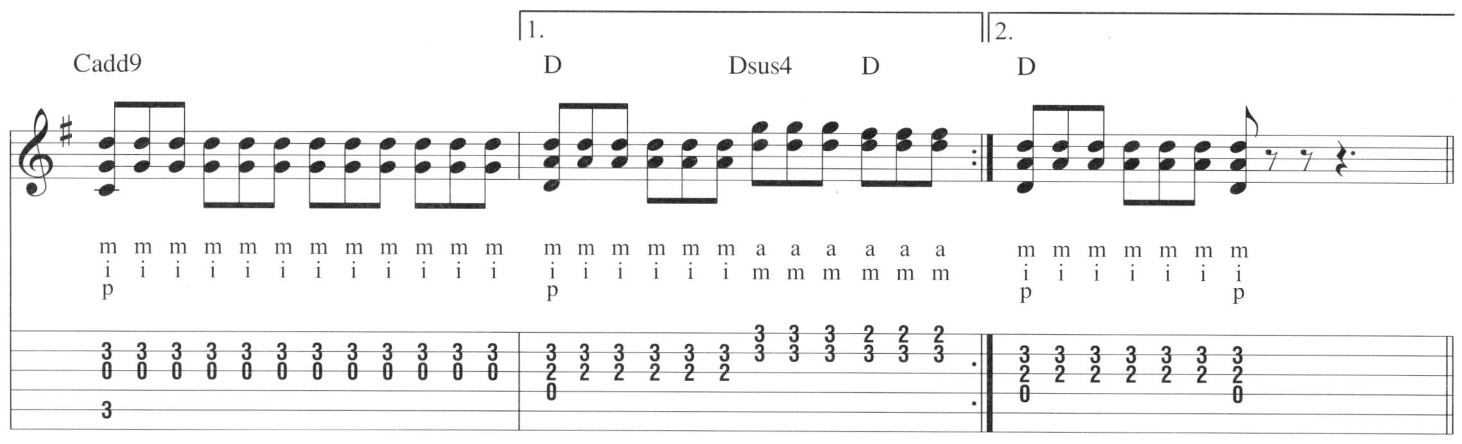

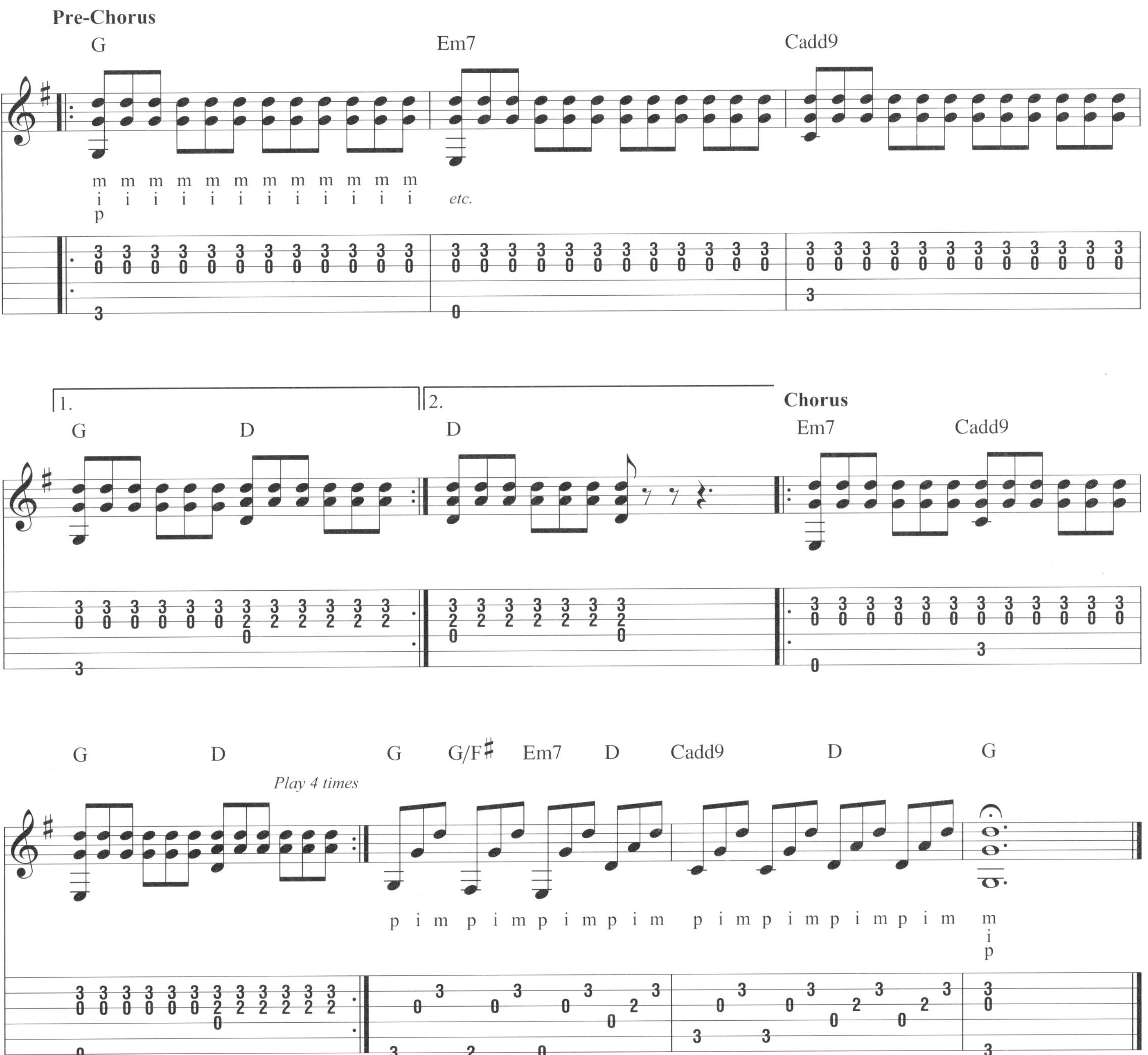

FINGERSTYLE SOLO ARRANGEMENTS

So far, we've been playing fingerstyle accompaniment patterns. We can also play solo guitar arrangements that include both the accompaniment and the melody. Advanced versions of this style can get very complicated, combining difficult chords with melody notes and harmony. But for our purpose, we'll take a simpler approach and combine melody notes with bass notes. And to make it even easier while we're learning how to do this, all the bass notes in our first song will be open strings! Pluck the bass notes with your thumb, and use whichever fingers you like for the melody notes. Note that this song is in the key of A major, which uses three sharps in the key signature.

SILENT NIGHT

Traditional

Now let's take a melody we learned in the first chapter, "Ode to Joy," and add some bass notes to it. This time, the bass notes will be fretted, so the arrangement will be a bit more difficult than the last one. We want to let those bass notes ring for the full measure, so be careful not to pick up your finger. It will take some time and concentration to train one finger to continue fretting a note while other fingers change. This is the real challenge in playing solo guitar, but it's worth the effort, as the effect can sound like two different guitars playing at the same time. Note that in order to keep those bass notes ringing, we'll need to use our pinky to fret the melody notes on fret 3.

ODE TO JOY

Ludwig van Beethoven

TRAVIS PICKING

Merle Travis, the legendary country guitarist, popularized a fingerstyle technique now known as Travis picking. *Travis picking* involves using the thumb to play steady alternating bass notes, while the fingers add a syncopated melody on top. Let's try a simple Travis-picking pattern on some Am and Em chords. Pay close attention to the right-hand fingering and take it very slow at first. Once the pattern becomes comfortable and feels almost automatic, you'll be able to build speed.

EXERCISE 48

Here's another Travis-picking pattern to try. Note that this one involves plucking two strings at the same time. The exercise will also give you a little more practice with the F chord. Also keep in mind that, for the F chord, you'll need to shift your right-hand fingers to a higher set of strings to pick the right notes. There are countless Travis-picking patterns, but the signature style is the alternating bass notes played by the thumb.

EXERCISE 49

Now let's put our Travis-picking skills to use for the final song of the chapter, Fleetwood Mac's classic, "Landslide." Throughout the song, the thumb plucks the bottom three strings, the index finger covers the third string, the middle finger the second string, and the ring finger the first. Check out the new chords you'll be playing, shown above the beginning of the piece. Am7 is shaped just like a C chord but without the C on the fifth string. It's been a while since we've seen them, but we also have a few "slash chords," G/B and D/F# (pronounced "G over B" and "D over F#"). Again, these are simply chords where the bass note, the lowest note in the chord, is different than the one we normally use. If you want to play along with the original recording, you'll need a capo on fret 3 (but no capo is needed to play along with our included audio).

LANDSLIDE

Words and Music by Stevie Nicks

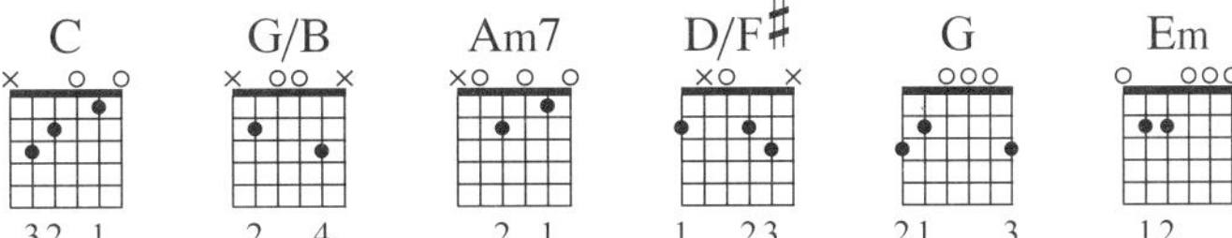

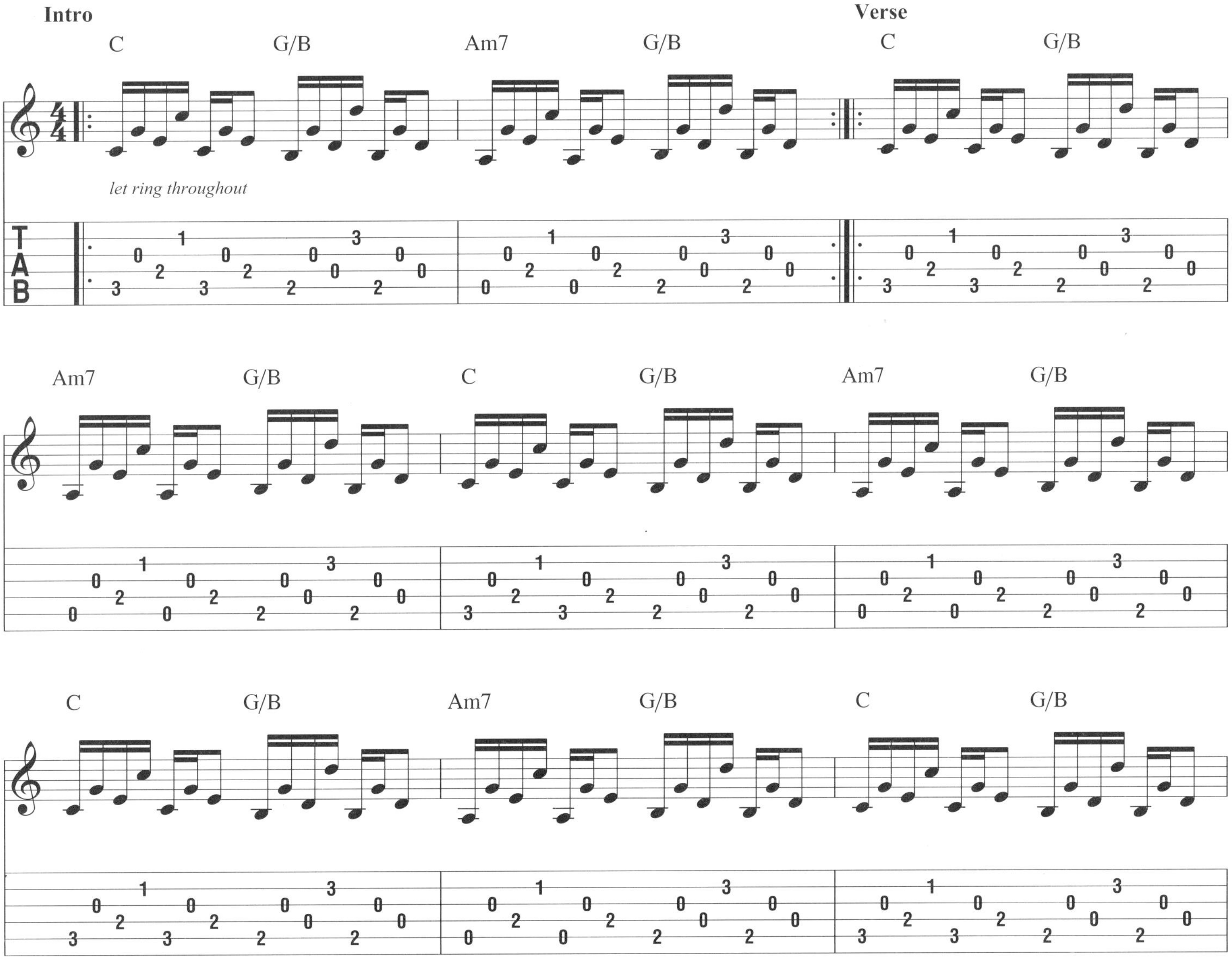

C
32 1
G/B
2 4
Am7
2 1
D/F#
1 23
G
21 3
Em
12

Intro
C
G/B
Am7
G/B
Verse
C
G/B
let ring throughout
Am7
G/B
C
G/B
Am7
G/B
C
G/B
Am7
G/B
C
G/B

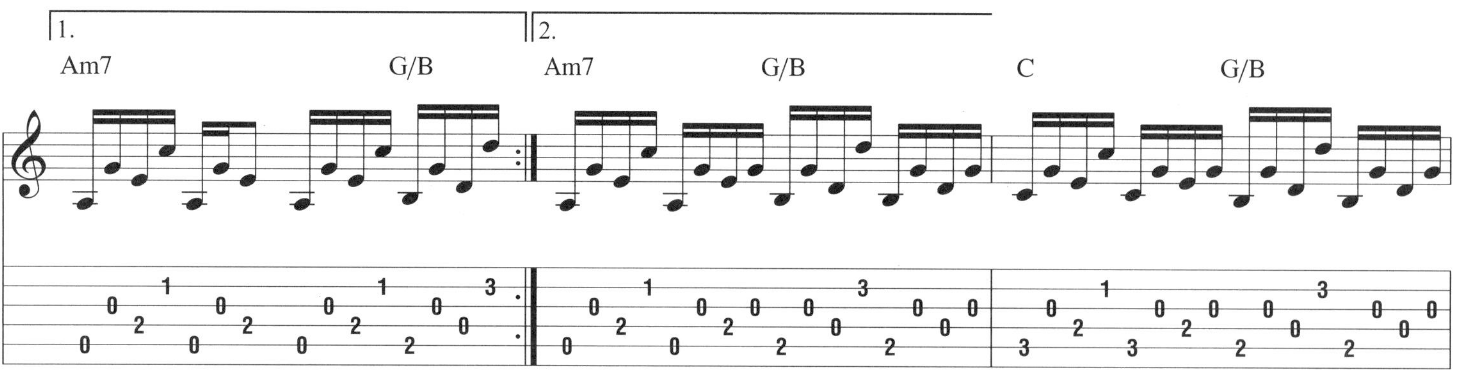
1.
2.
Am7
G/B
Am7
G/B
C
G/B

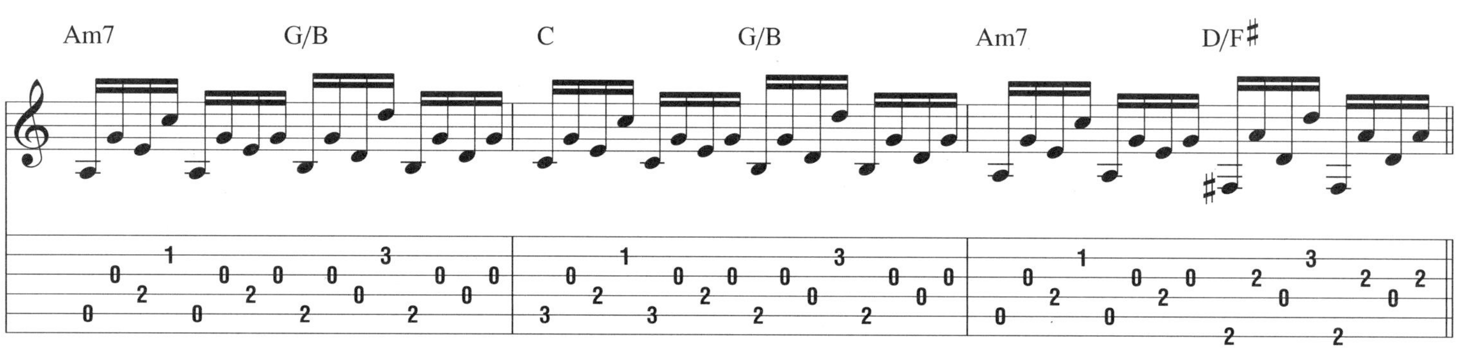
Am7
G/B
C
G/B
Am7
D/F♯

Chorus
G
D/F♯
Em
C
G/B

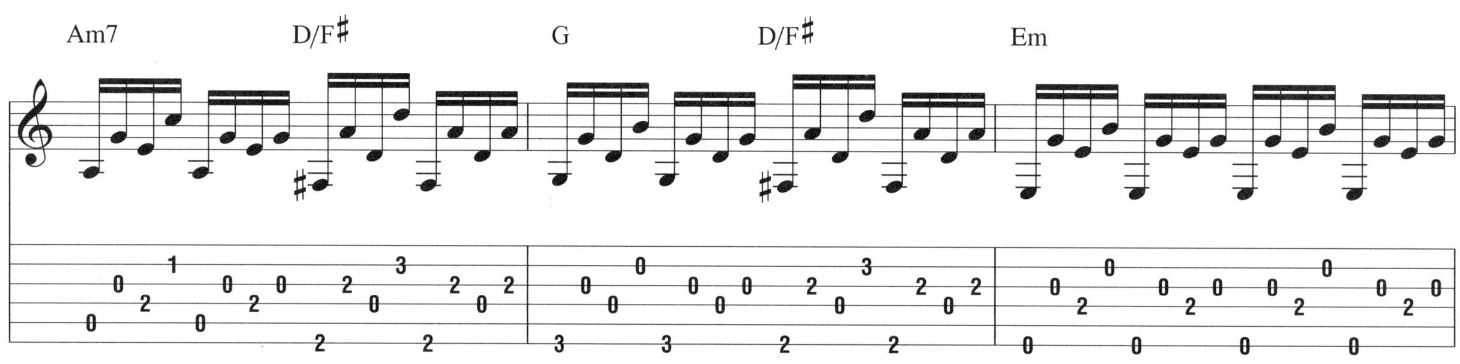
Am7
D/F♯
G
D/F♯
Em

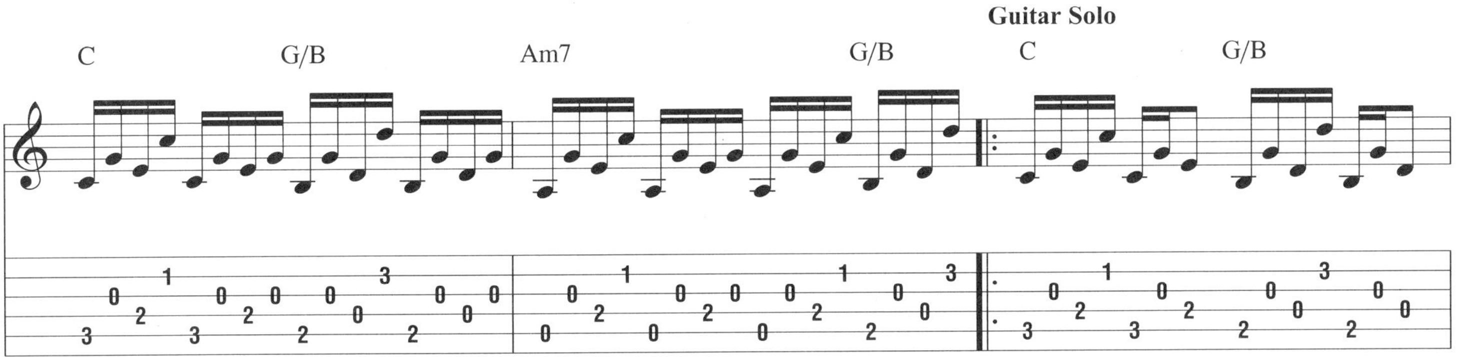
Guitar Solo
C
G/B
Am7
G/B
C
G/B

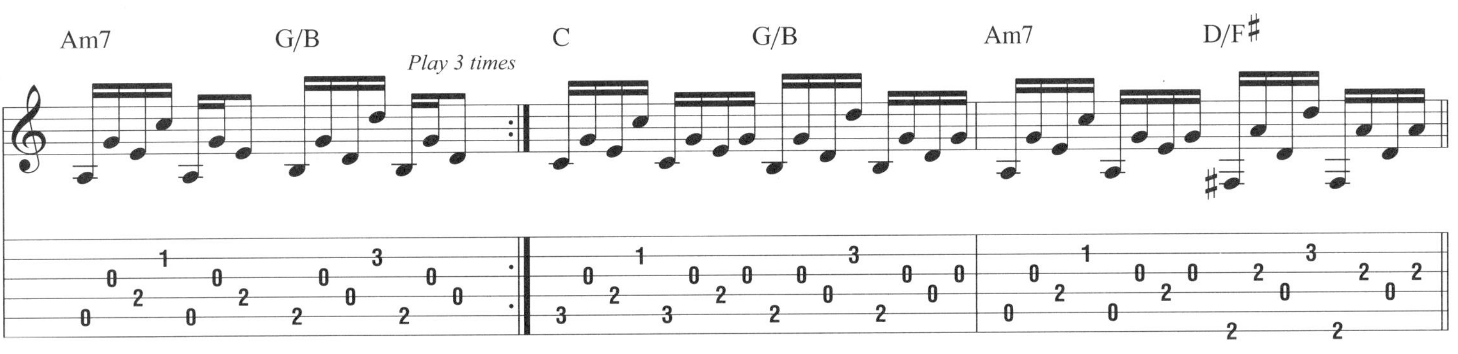
Am7
G/B
Play 3 times
C
G/B
Am7
D/F♯

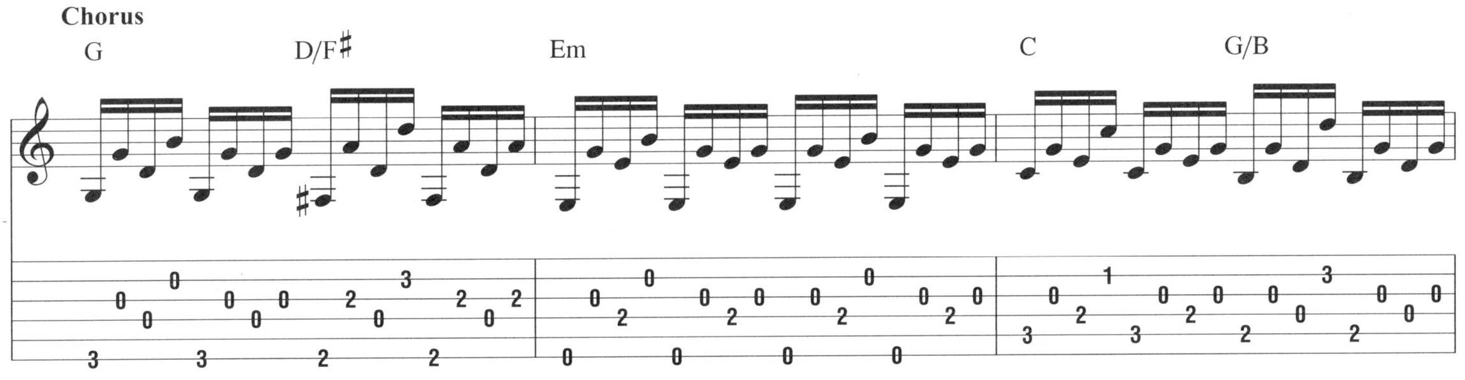
Chorus
G
D/F♯
Em
C
G/B

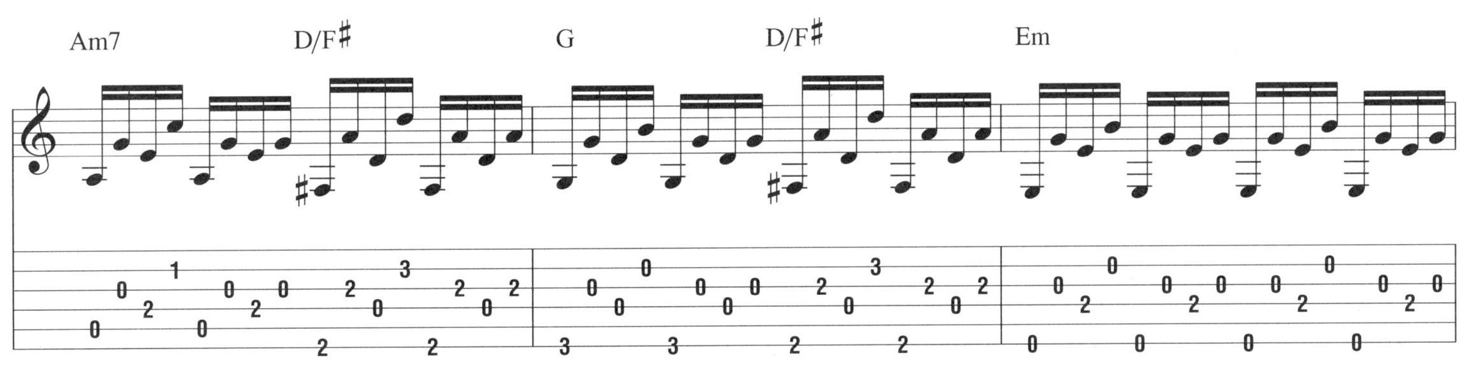
Am7
D/F♯
G
D/F♯
Em

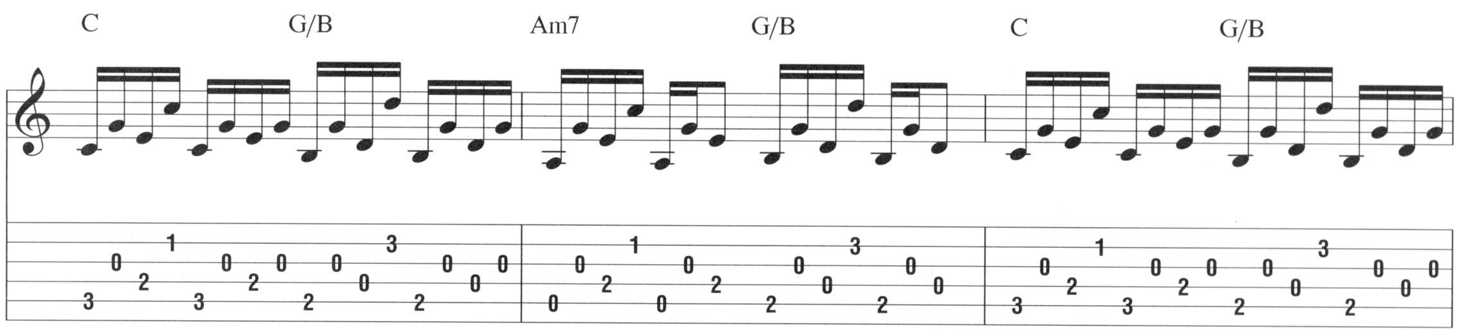
C
G/B
Am7
G/B
C
G/B

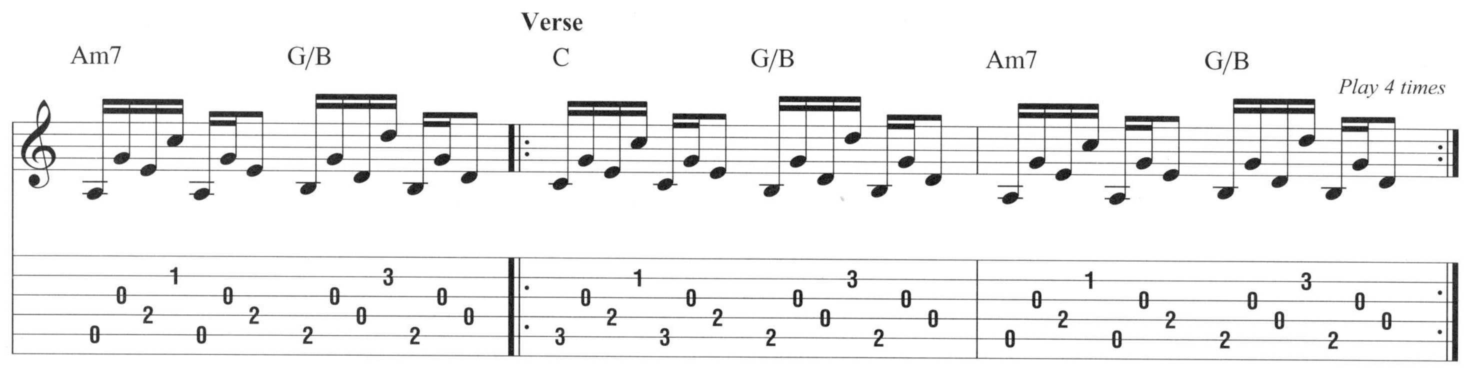
Verse
Am7
G/B
C
G/B
Am7
G/B
Play 4 times

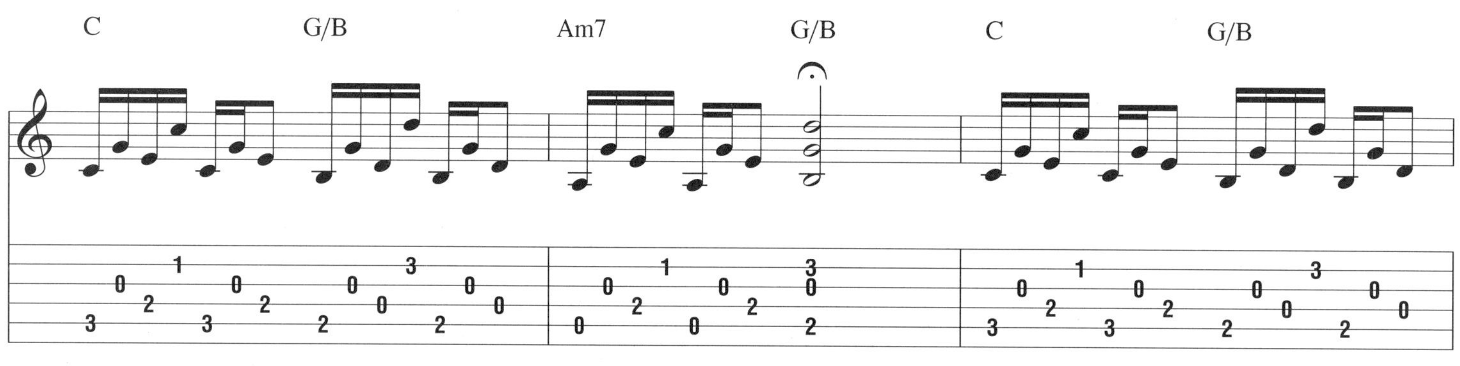
C
G/B
Am7
G/B
C
G/B

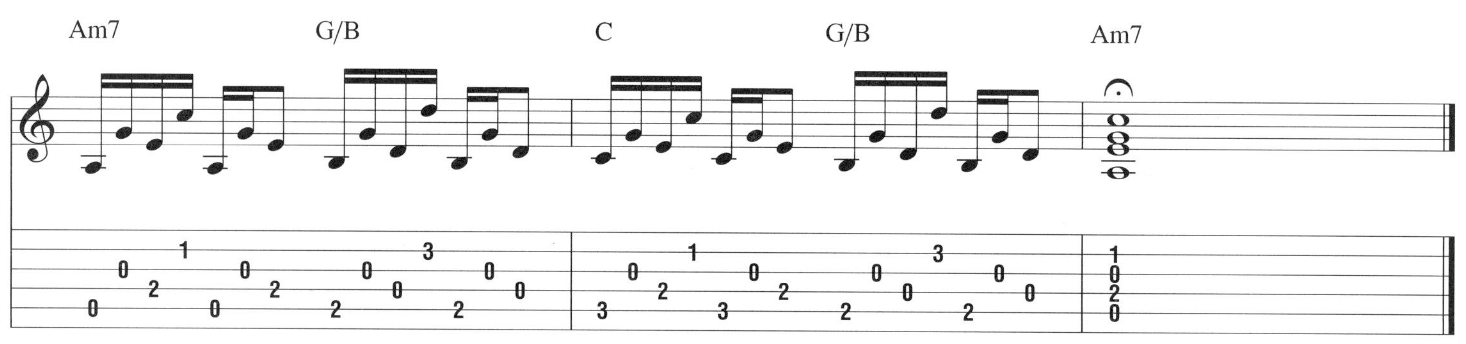
Am7
G/B
C
G/B
Am7

CHAPTER 8: BARRE CHORDS

You've already gotten a taste of barre chords with that F chord we've been using. In this chapter, we'll learn the most commonly used barre chord shapes: major, minor, and dominant 7th. A *barre chord* is simply a chord that includes a barre. Every type of barre chord we're going to learn will include two different shapes, one rooted on the sixth string and one rooted on the fifth string. Although very challenging at first, these will open up the door to being able to play almost any chord anywhere on the neck.

Before we try and tackle our first barre chord, let's try just barring all six strings with our first finger on fret 3. Lay it across flat, keeping it straight and close to the fret, and make sure you have good thumb support behind the neck. Play each note individually to make sure they're all ringing clearly. It can sometimes be helpful to roll your first finger ever so slightly towards the nut if you're having trouble fretting and hearing all the notes.

EXERCISE 50

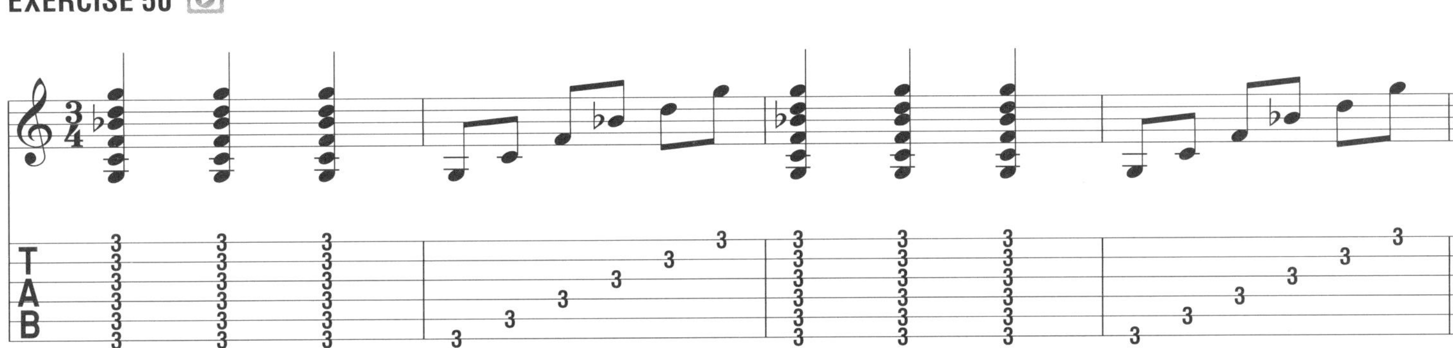

It will take some time and repetition to build up the strength and dexterity needed to barre all six strings cleanly, but it will be well worth the effort!

"E SHAPE" BARRE CHORDS

Let's take a look at the barre chords rooted on the sixth string first. We sometimes refer to these as "E shape" barre chords, since what we're doing is taking an open E major chord shape, moving it up the neck, and using our first finger to fret what were previously open notes.

In the following exercise, first play the open E major chord using your middle, ring, and pinky fingers, as shown in the chord chart (don't use the usual open E fingering). Then move all of those fingers up one fret and lay your first finger across all six strings at fret 1. This will be an F major barre chord. If you look closely at the diagram for this chord, you should be able to see that what we're doing is combining the open F chord with the F5 power chord. Remember to keep that first finger straight and flat while still keeping the other fingers curved and fretting with the fingertips.

EXERCISE 51

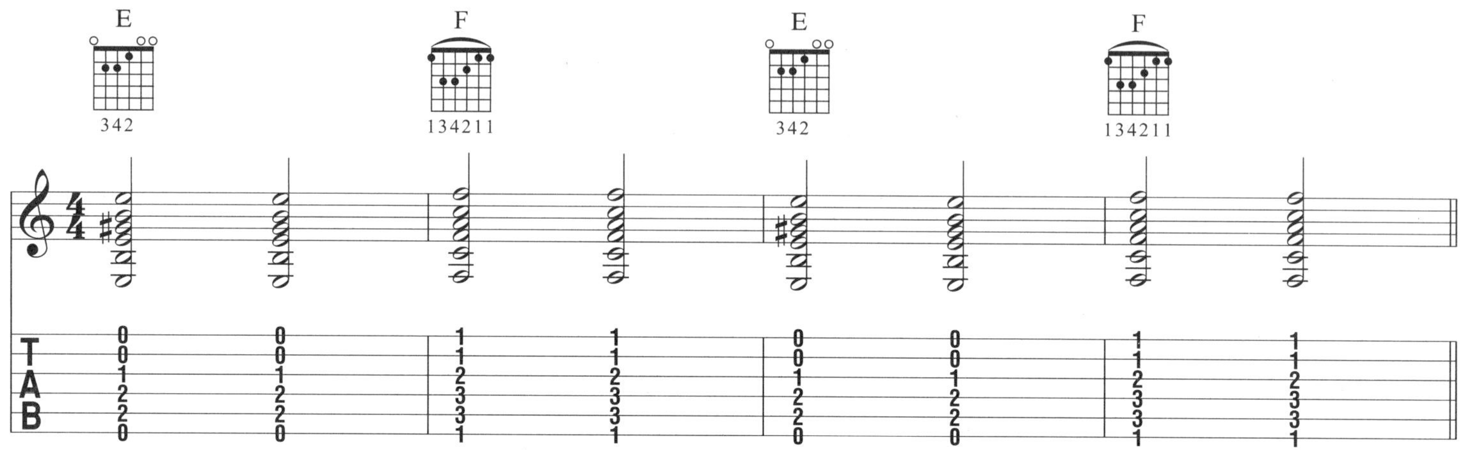

Now let's take that F major chord and move it up two frets to get a G major chord rooted on fret 3.

EXERCISE 52

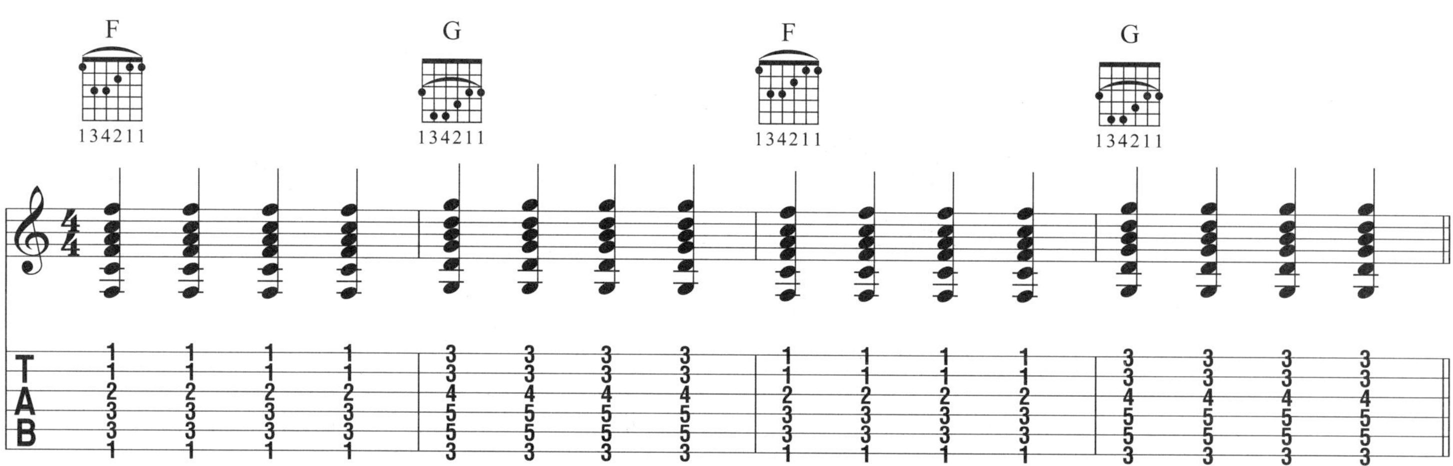

Are you noticing a pattern here? We can simply move this chord shape up and down the neck to get any major chord we need, defined by the root on the sixth string. So, if we need a G# major chord, simply move the root of the chord shape to fret 4. All barre chord shapes are thought of as "movable" because we can move them all around the neck.

"Em SHAPE" BARRE CHORDS

To get minor barre chords rooted on the sixth string, all we need to do is take our second finger off of the "E shape" barre chord. For example, here's what an F♯m barre chord looks like.

Let's put what we know about barre chords to use on the chorus of Adele's hit, "Rolling in the Deep."

ROLLING IN THE DEEP

Words and Music by Adele Adkins
and Paul Epworth

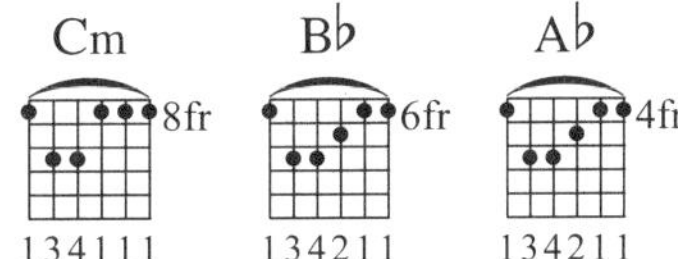

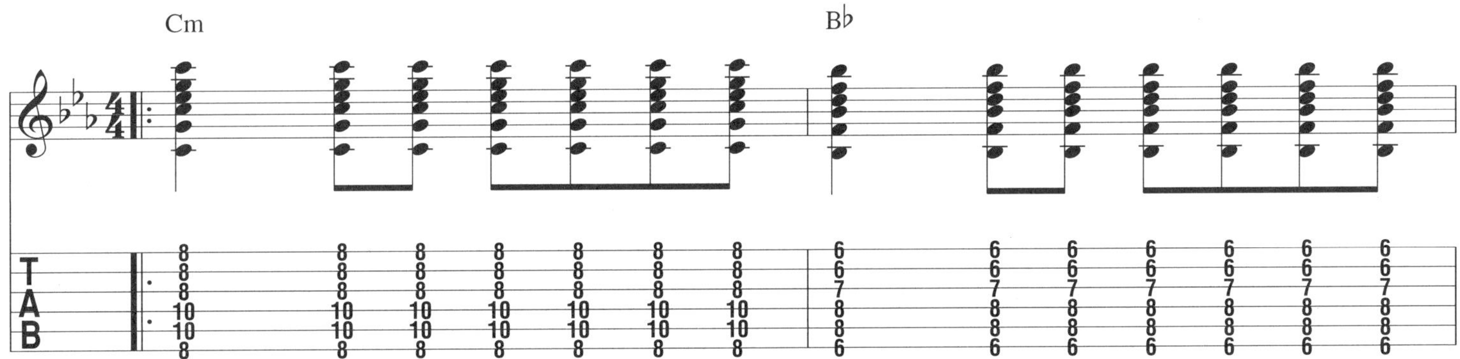

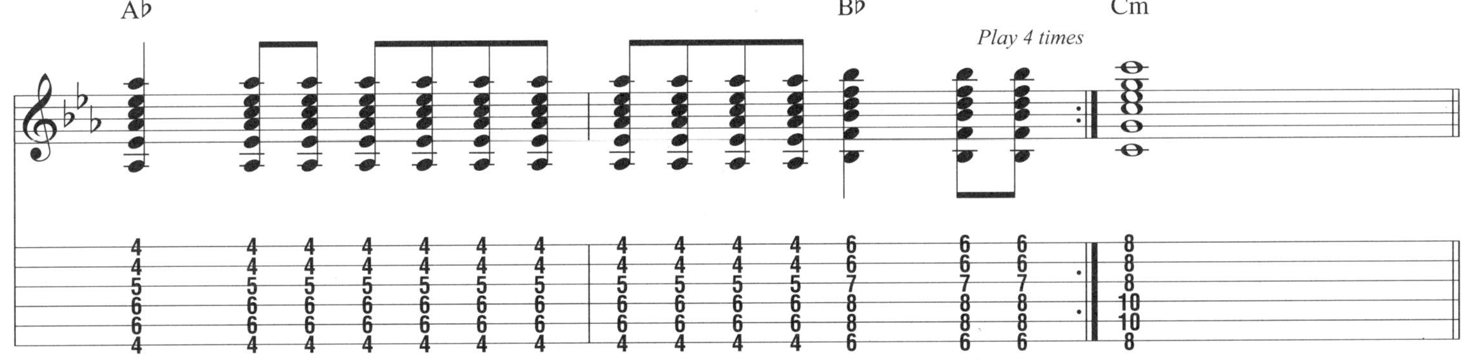

"A SHAPE" BARRE CHORDS

Now let's take a look at the barre chords rooted on the fifth string. We'll refer to these as "A shape" barre chords since they're based on the open A major chord shape. There are two different ways to play this barre chord shape. One way is to use your middle, ring, and pinky fingers to play the notes not included in the barre. But the more common way is to use your third finger to barre those notes and just disregard playing the first string. When using the second approach, we don't need to barre with the first finger, just the third. For the third-finger barre, many players find it useful to add the second finger on top of the third finger for some added support. Take a look here at the B♭ major barre chord, for example.

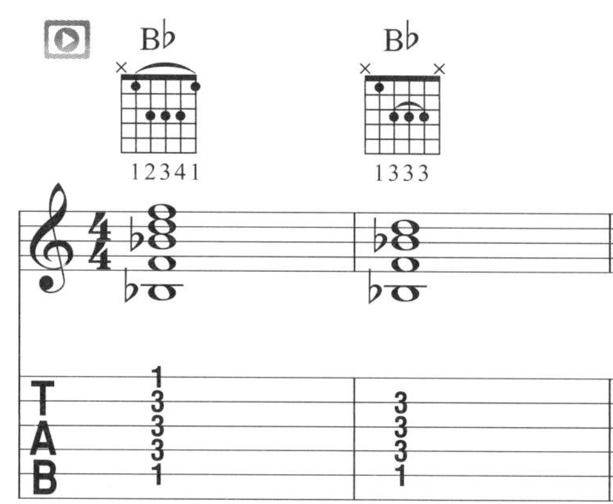

In the next exercise, let's try moving around this A major shape to get a few new barre chords. If you'd like, you can also use the first fingering option for these chords and include the first string.

EXERCISE 53

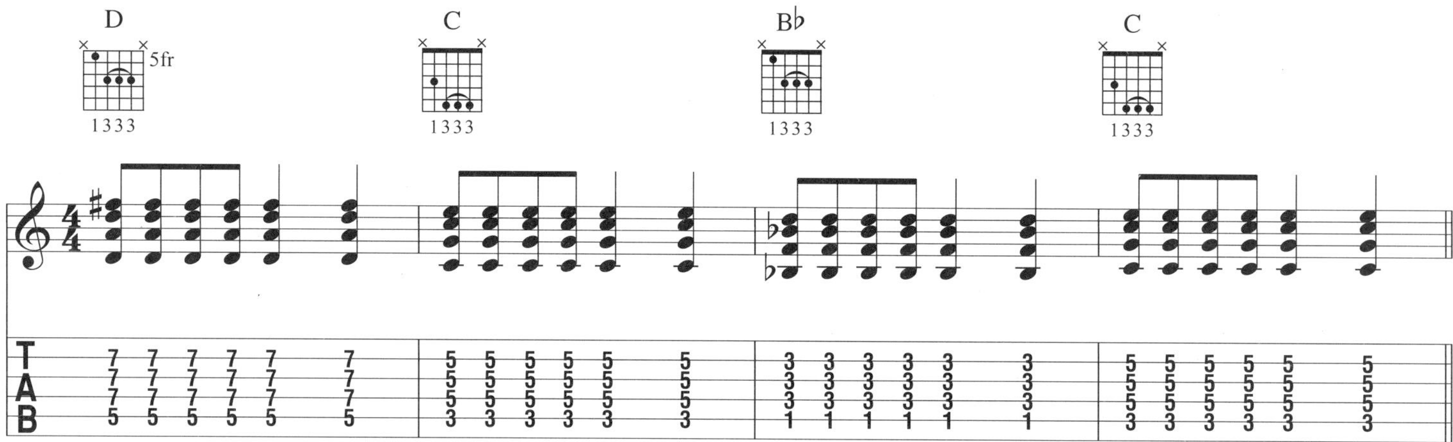

Now that you know the major barre chord shapes with sixth- and fifth-string roots, let's revisit the intro to "Smells Like Teen Spirit," where we previously just used power chords. Again, recognize those power chord shapes within the full barre chords.

SMELLS LIKE TEEN SPIRIT

Words and Music by Kurt Cobain,
David Grohl, and Krist Novoselic

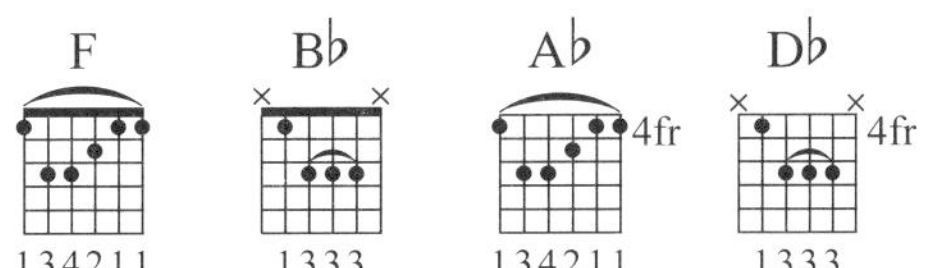

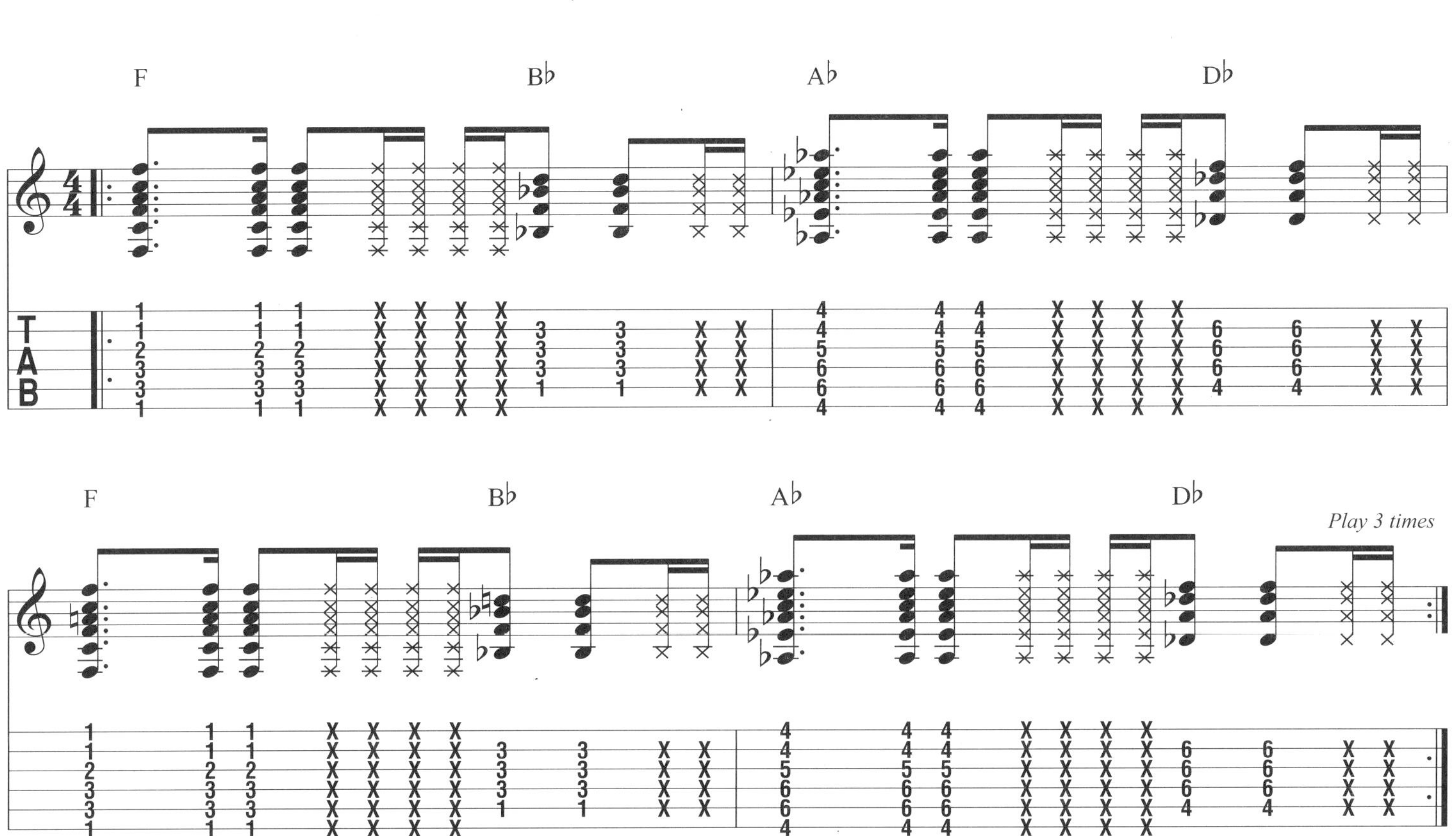

"Am SHAPE" BARRE CHORDS

For the minor barre chord shape that's rooted on the fifth string, we'll use the open Am shape. So, fret that Am with the middle, ring, and pinky, and then move it up and add the first-finger barre. Try it here, going from Am to Bm.

EXERCISE 54

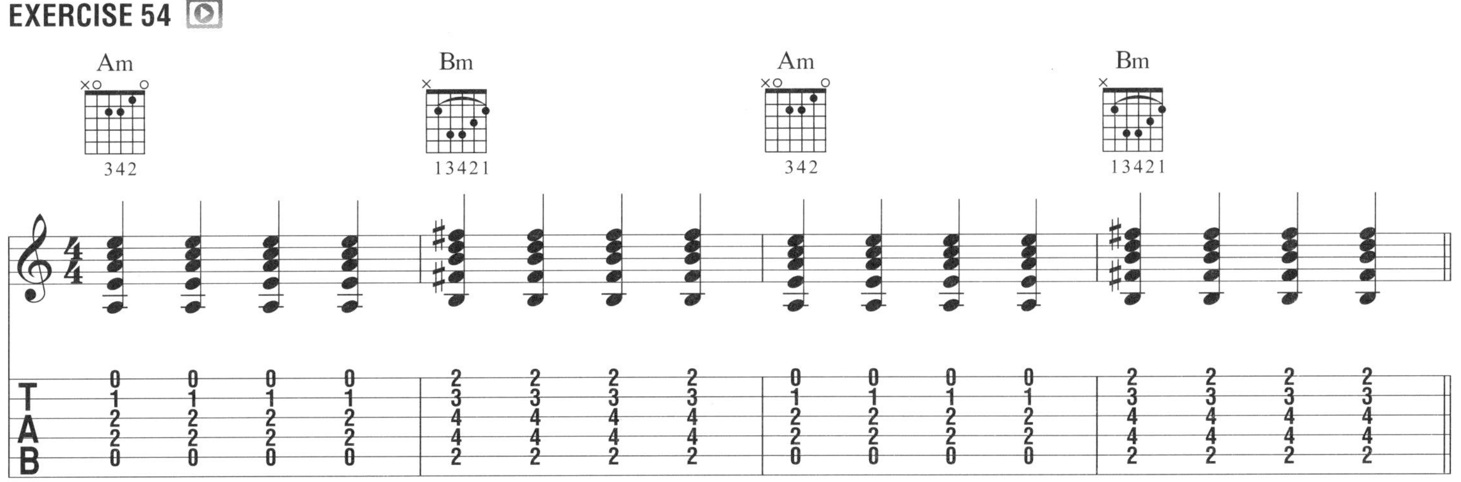

Now that you know your major and minor barre chord shapes rooted on both the sixth and fifth strings, let's put a few of them together in a popular progression.

EXERCISE 55

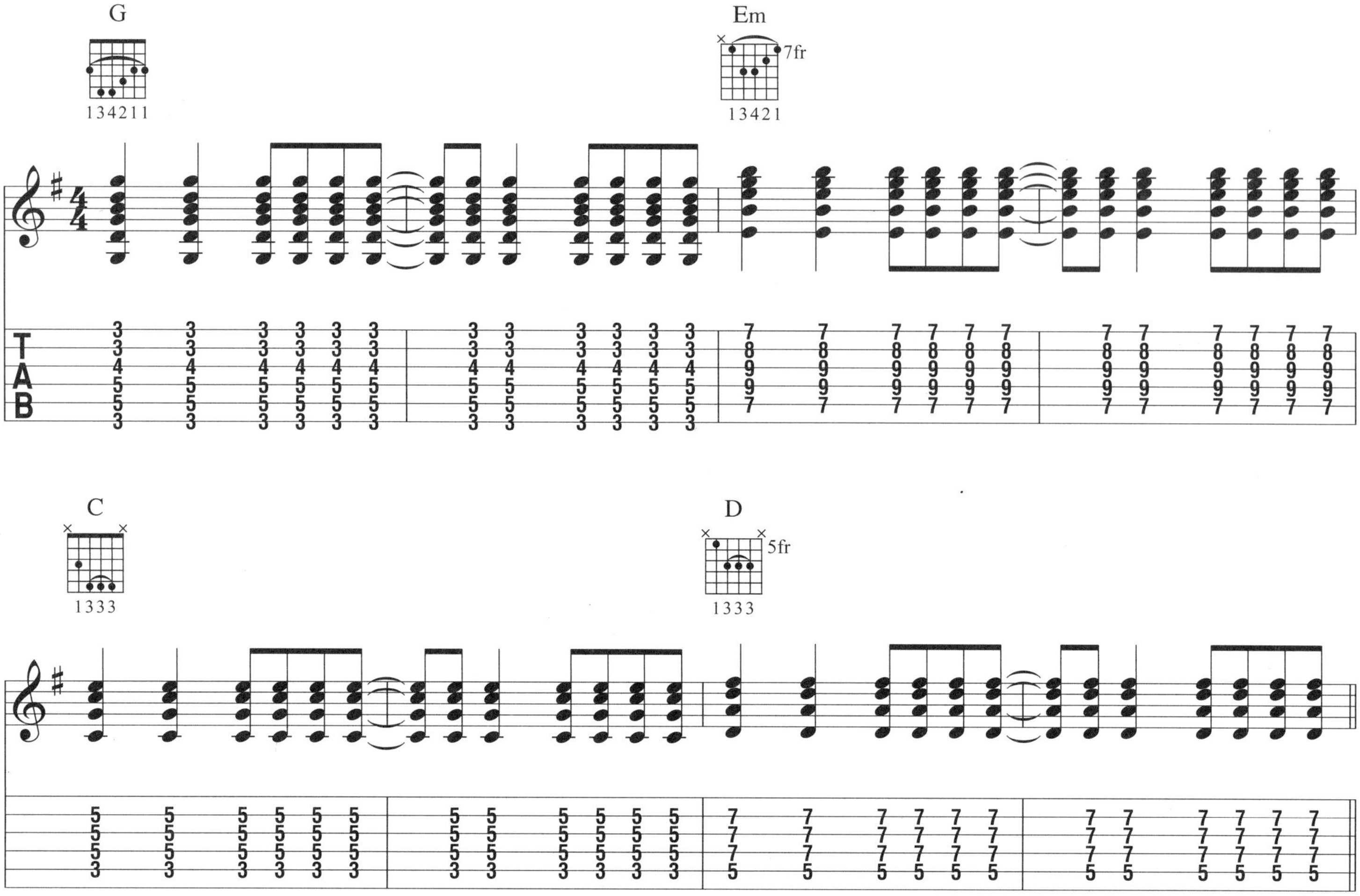

G
134211
Em
7fr
13421
C
1333
D
5fr
1333

"DOMINANT 7TH SHAPE" BARRE CHORDS

Finally, let's take a look at the dominant 7th barre chord shapes on both the sixth- and fifth-string roots. Notice their similarity to the major barre chord shapes. As with all other barre chords, these shapes can be moved to different spots on the fretboard to get other dominant 7th chords.

EXERCISE 56

G7
131211
C7
13141

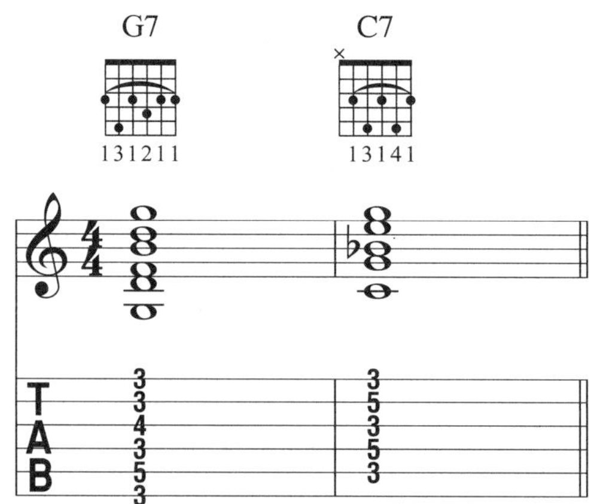

We'll close out this chapter, as well as the book, with the popular tune "I'm Yours" by Jason Mraz. Don't worry about strumming the exact number of strings notated, but rather aim for those strings in general and keep a steady and relaxed strum pattern going. Instead of playing a straight sixteenth-note pattern, we'll use a *swing feel*, which basically means that the first sixteenth note in every group of two will be held a little longer than the second one. Listen to the included audio to get a feel for this rhythm.

Words and Music by Jason Mraz

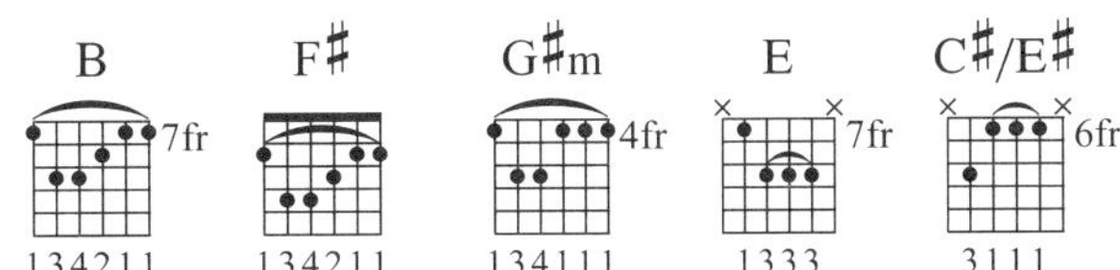

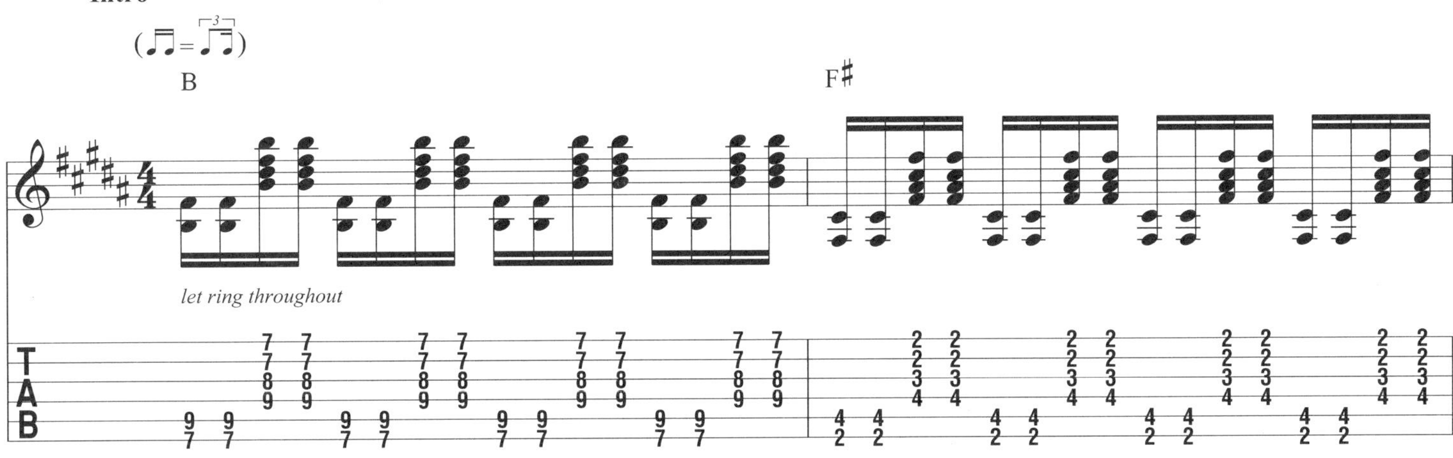

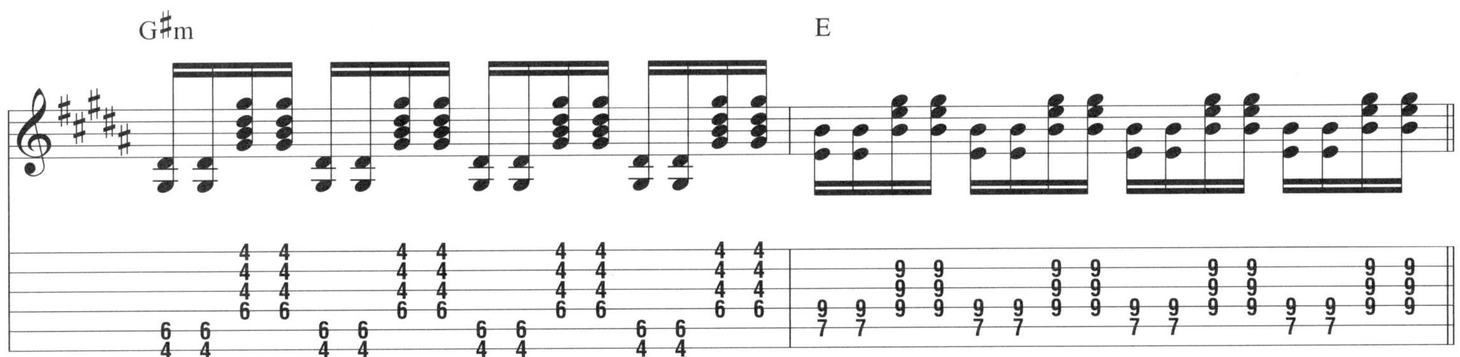

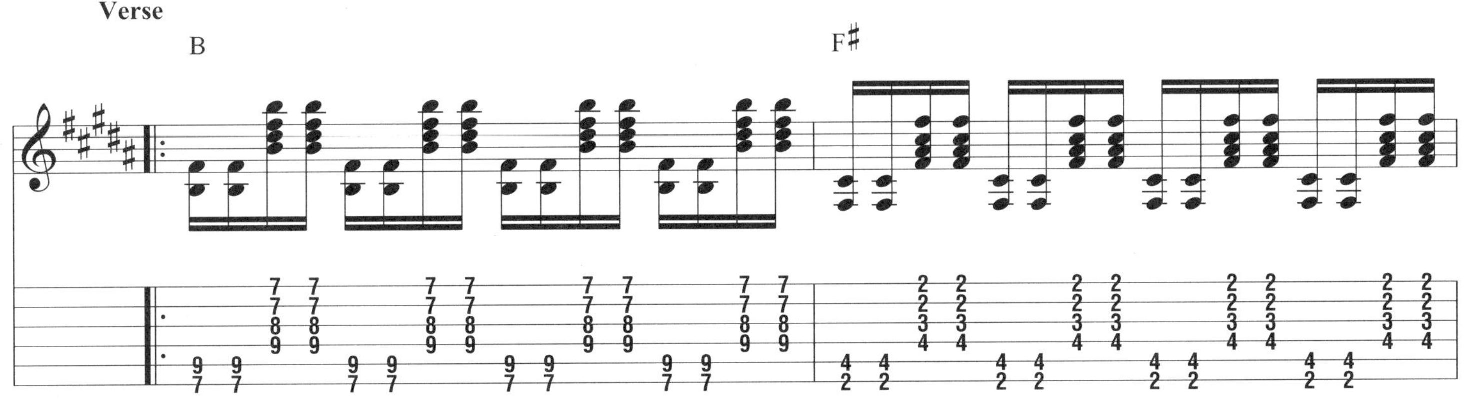

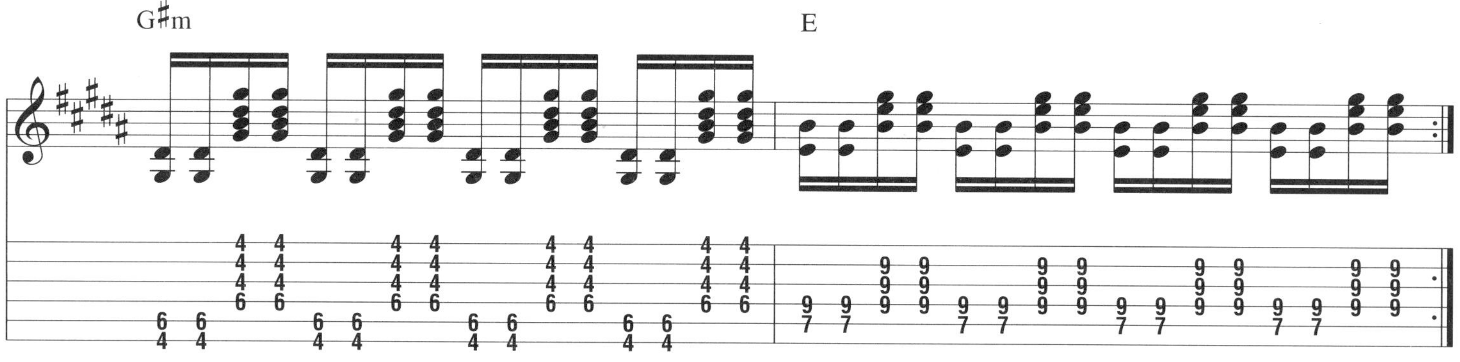

Chorus

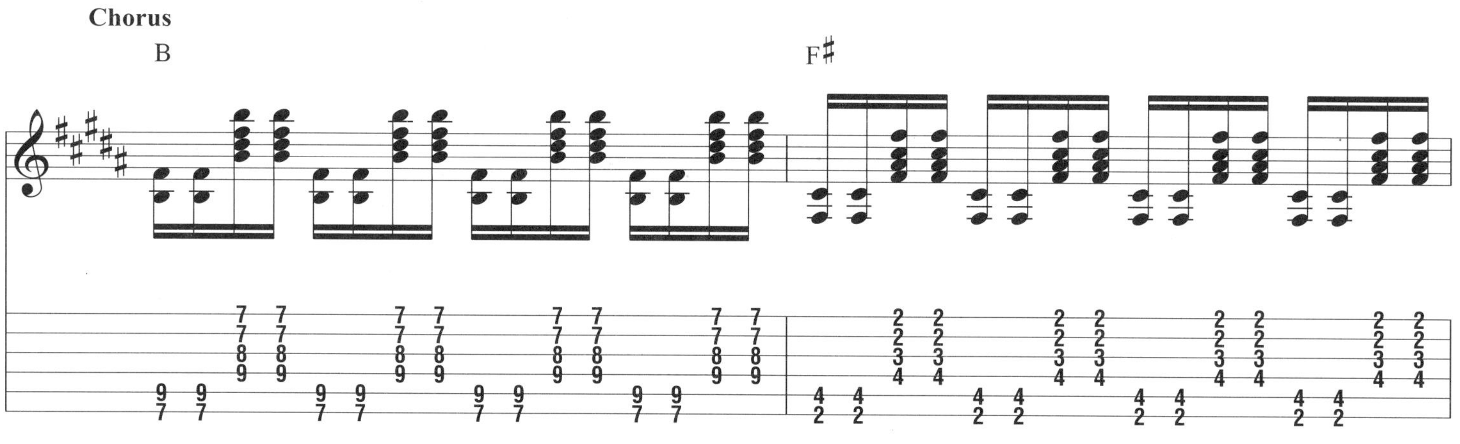

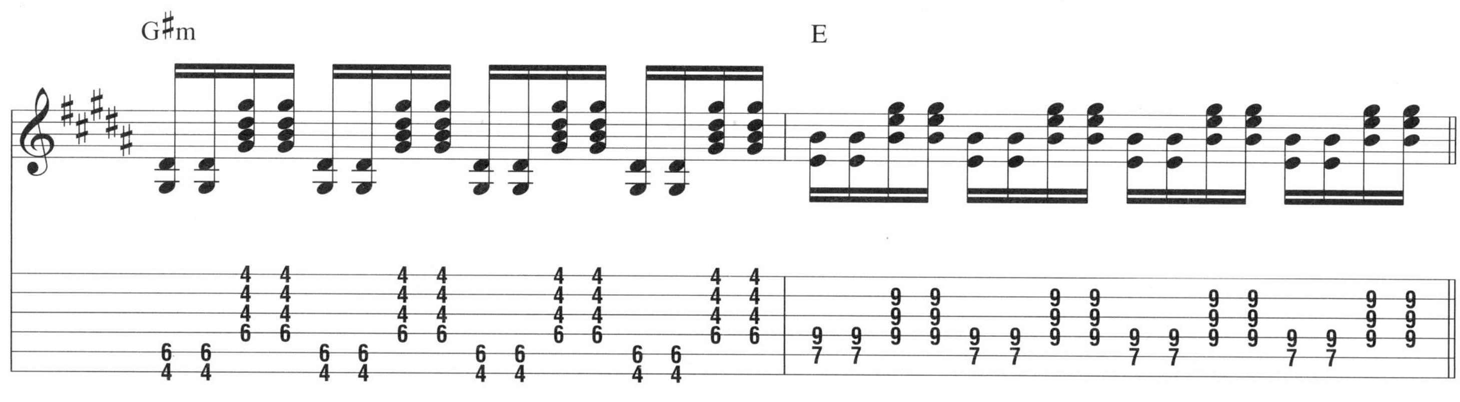

Interlude

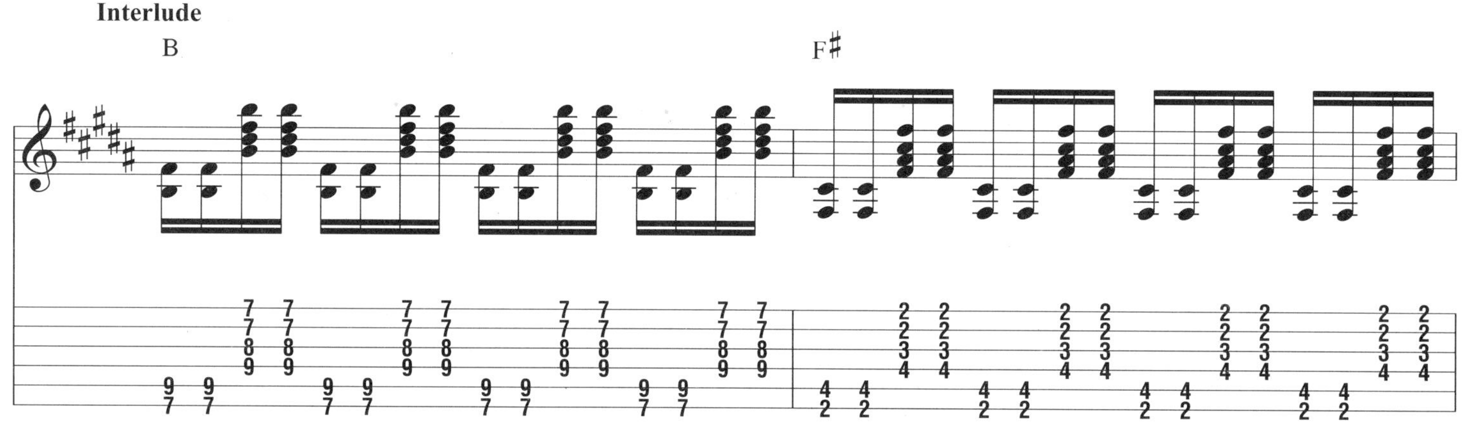

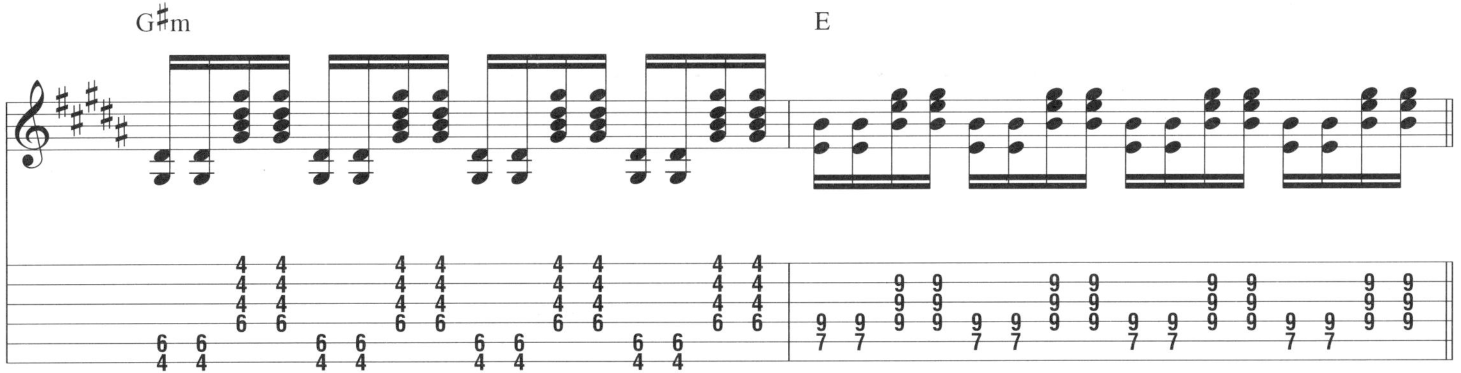
G♯m
E

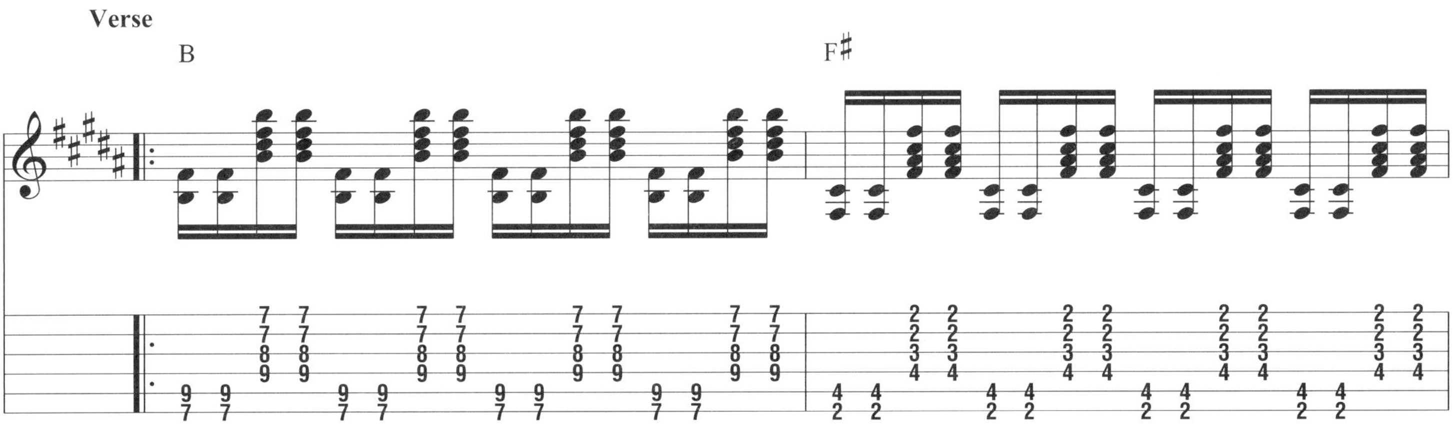
Verse
B
F♯

G♯m
E
C♯/E♯

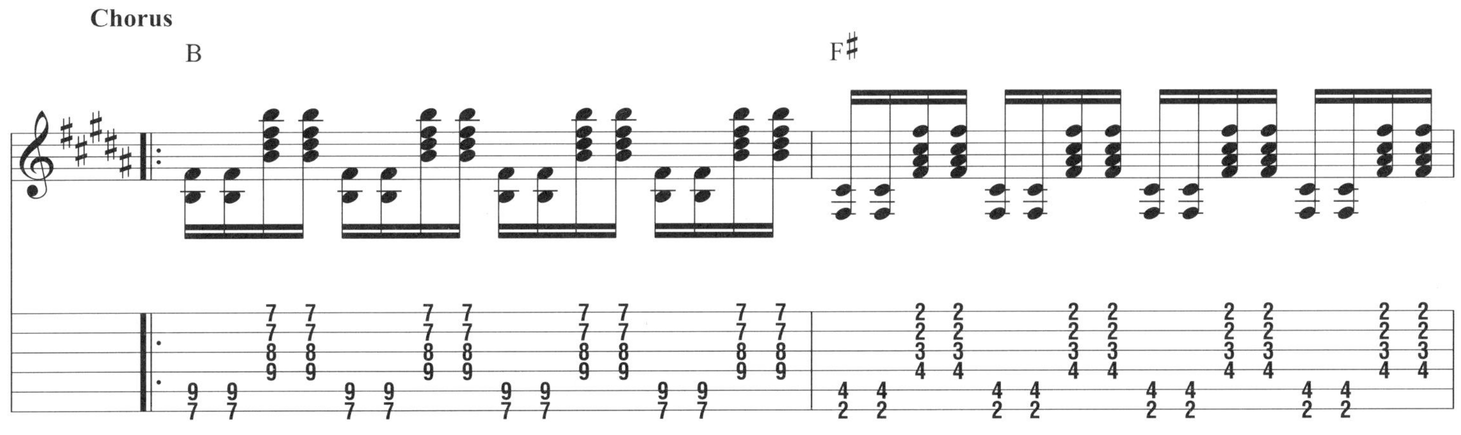
Chorus
B
F♯

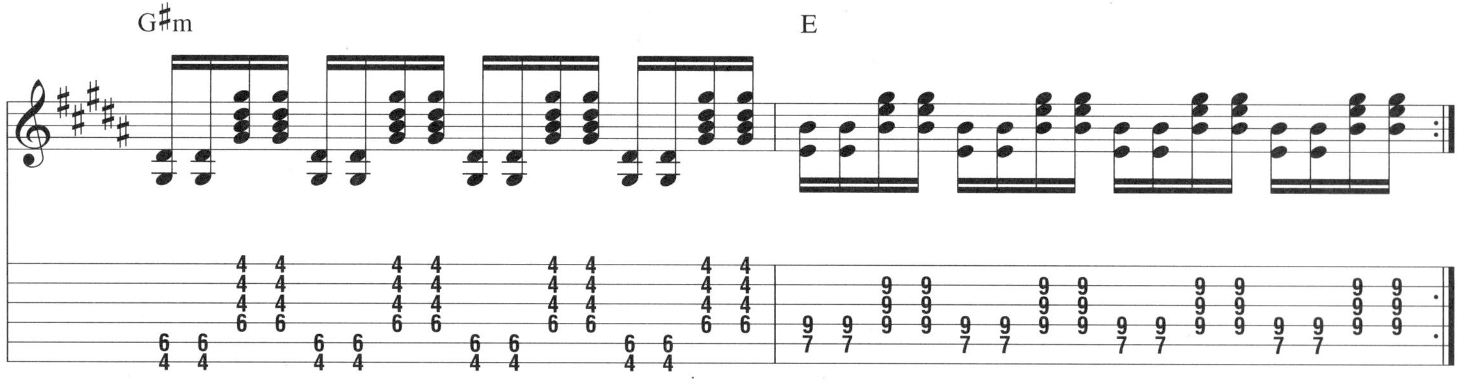
G♯m
E

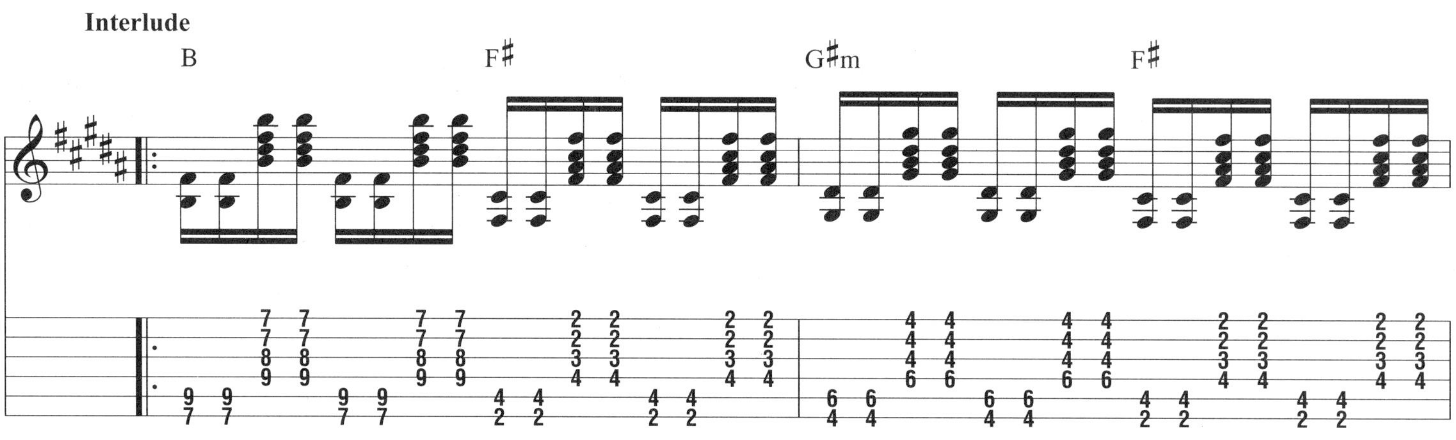
Interlude
B
F♯
G♯m
F♯

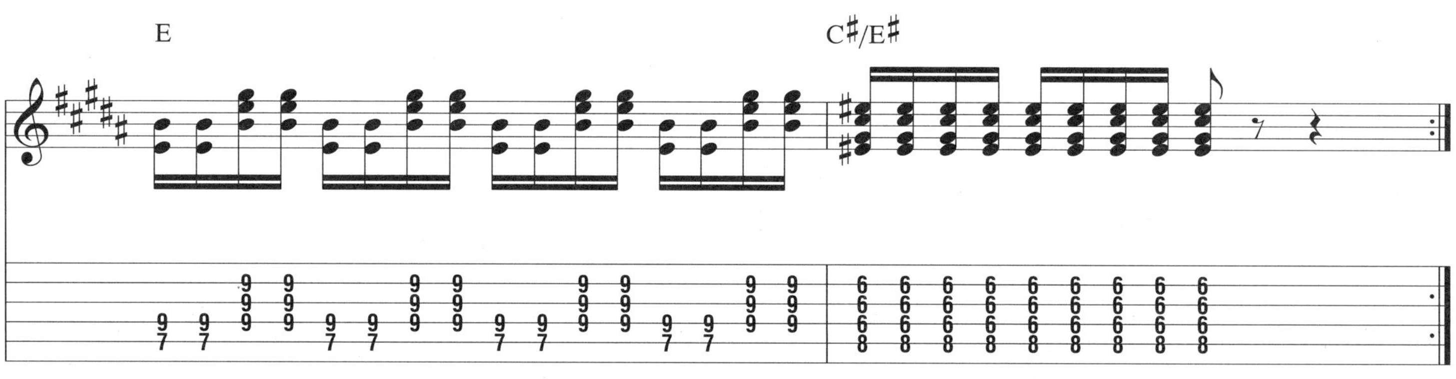
E
C♯/E♯

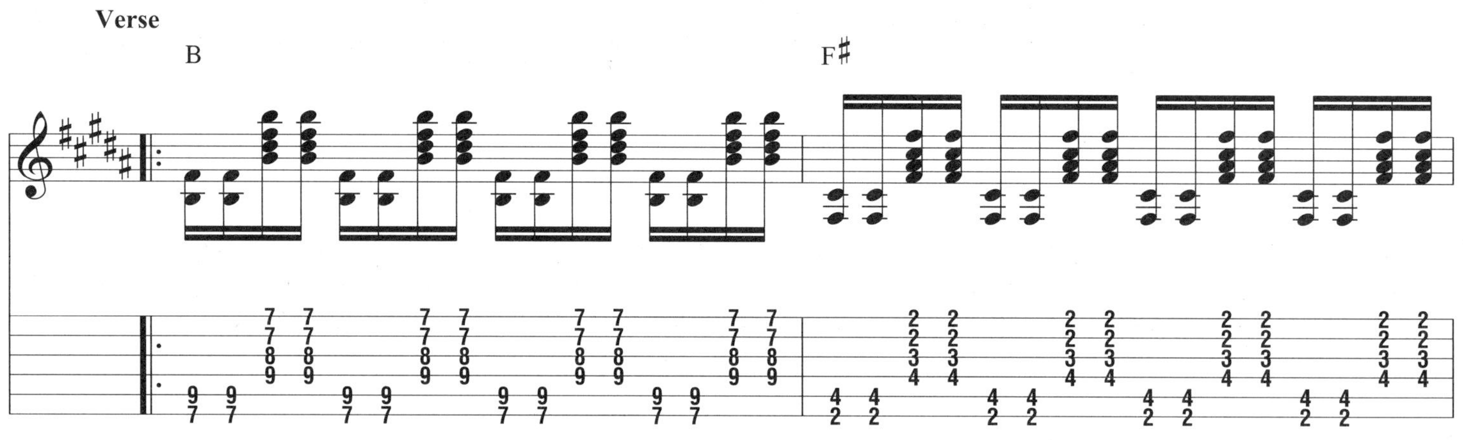
Verse
B
F♯

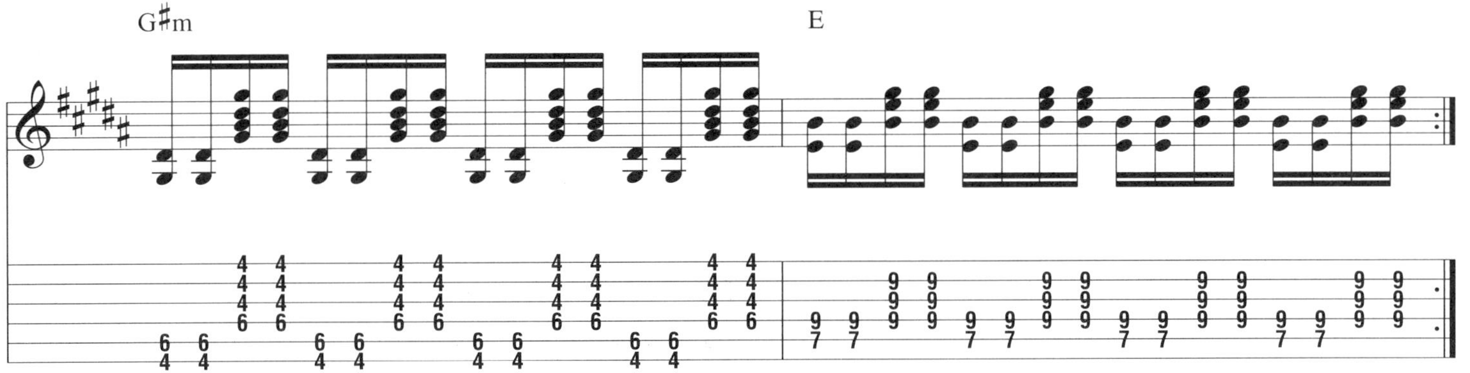
G♯m
E

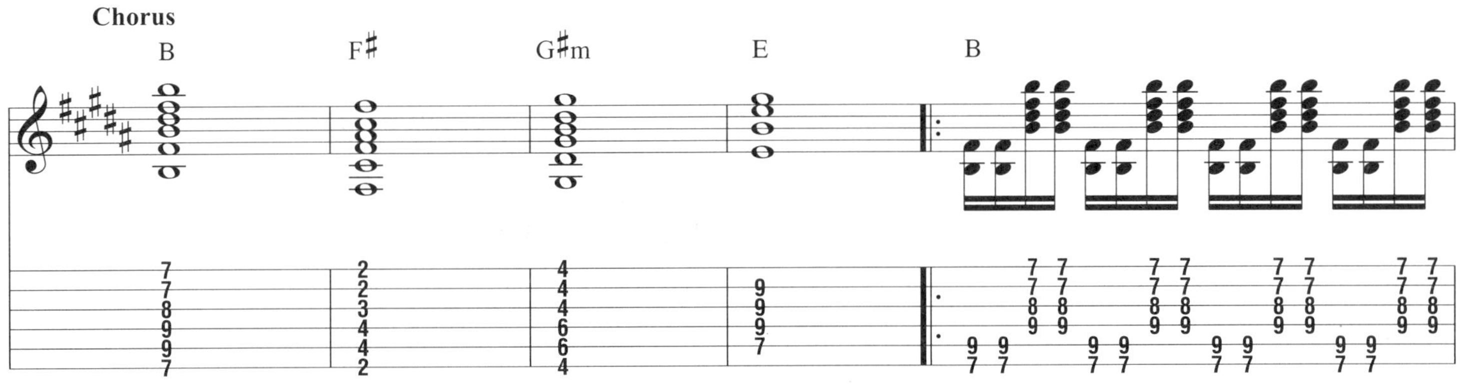
Chorus
B
F♯
G♯m
E
B

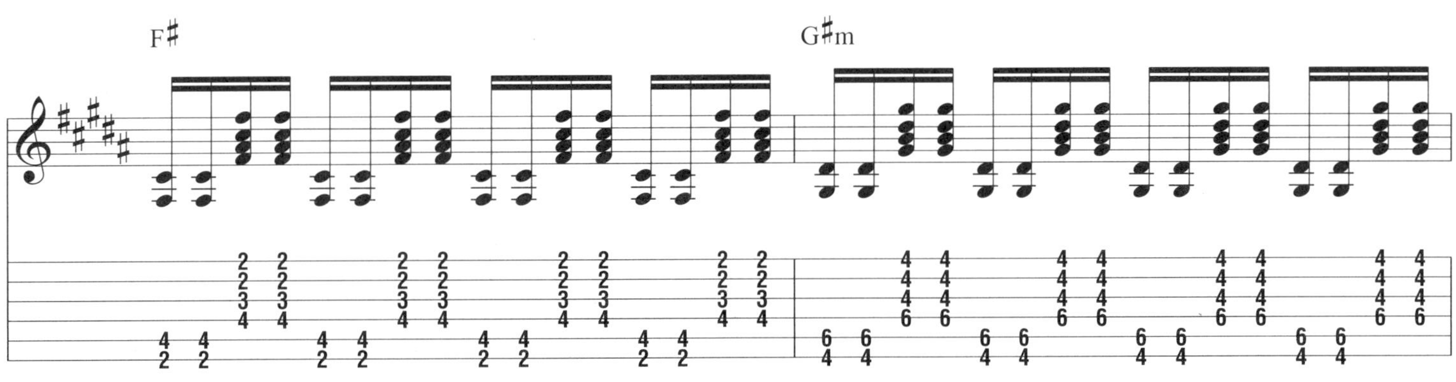
F♯
G♯m

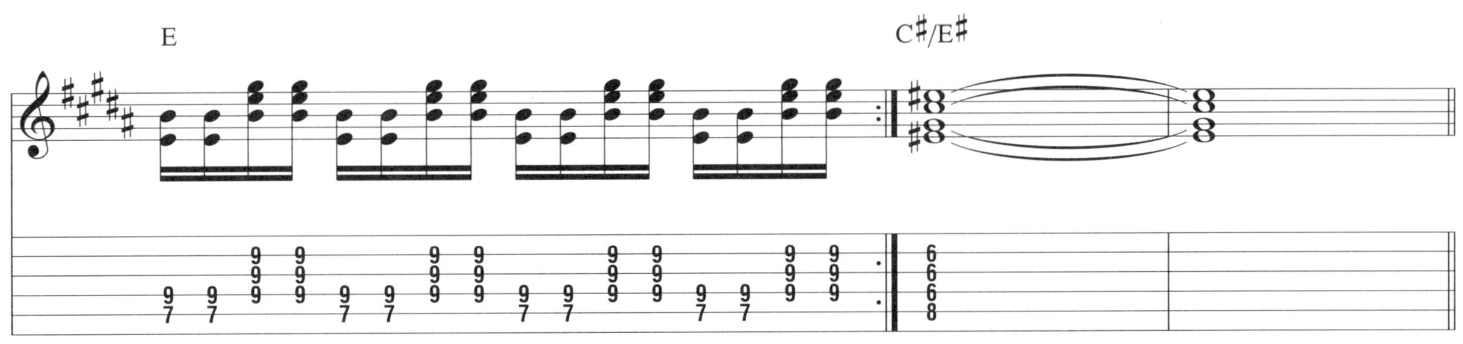
E
C♯/E♯

Outro

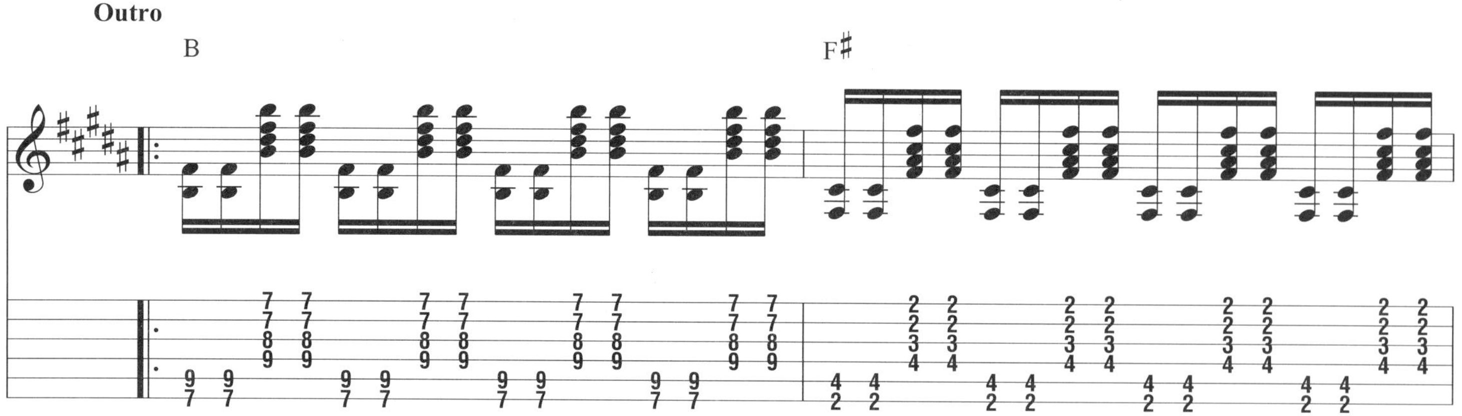

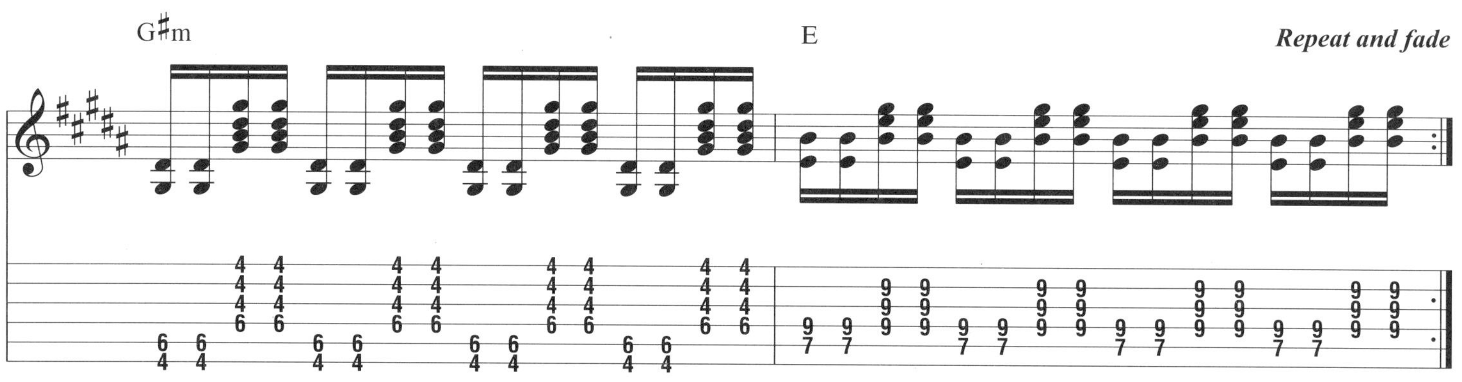